DIAMONDS ON THE ROAD

Peter C. Bruechle

Copyright 2020 © Peter C. Bruechle
All rights reserved. This book or any portion thereof may not
be reproduced or used in any manner whatsoever without the
express written permission of the publisher except for the use
of brief quotations in a book review.

ISBN
Set in Times New Roman

Books by Peter Bruechle

Egotecture?

*Issues and Challenges: Matters for Consideration,
Discussion and Consensus*

Contents

A note to the reader. 6

Chapter 1. On the Road Again. 7

Chapter 2. Why This Book? 9

Chapter 3. My Early Motorcycling Background.............................11

Chapter 4. My Dad and Further Motorcycling Background. 13

Chapter 5. Ewing Street, Welshpool and the United Nations at QPSS. 21

Chapter 6. Growing Up. 33

Chapter 7. The Wheat Belt..36

Chapter 8. Moving On and Up..41

Chapter 9. Europe and Civilisation. 49

Chapter 10. Home, Marriage and More Motorcycles. 51

Chapter 11. Across Oz on a Motorcycle for the First Time. 55

Chapter 12. The Motorcycling Environment. 57

Chapter 13. Across Australia Again. 59

Chapter 14. Nick's First Trip...64

Chapter 15. Around the North by BMW. 65

Chapter 16. Kaye on the Road. 69

Chapter 17. Hans on the Road...71

Chapter 18. Nick and I Plan a Trip..72

Chapter 19. Wally. 73

Chapter 20. Another Crash..77

Chapter 21. Nothing Daunted. 79

Chapter 22. Dubai. 81

Chapter 23. Choosing Kununurra. 83

Chapter 24. Day 1. Perth to Meekatharra. 85

Chapter 25. Day 2. Meekatharra to Munjina..................................90

Chapter 26. Day 3. Karajini Park. 92

Chapter 27. Day 4. Munjina to Broome. 100

Chapter 28. Day 5. Broome to Halls Creek. 104

Chapter 29. Day 6. Halls Creek – All Day. 108

Chapter 30. Day 7. Halls Creek to Purnululu................................110

Chapter 31. Day 8. Purnululu to Kununurra. 115

Chapter 32. Day 9. Around Kununurra. 120

Chapter 33. Day 10. Kununurra to El Questro..............................121

Chapter 34. Day 11. Around El Questro. 124

Chapter 35. Day 12. More El Questro and then Argyle. 127

Chapter 36. Day 13. At Argyle..137

Chapter 37. Day 14. The Ord River Trip...142

Chapter 38. Day 15. Argyle to Kununurra. 149

Chapter 39. Day 16. Kununurra to Wolf Creek Crater and back to Halls Creek..151

Chapter 40. Day 17. Halls Creek to Broome. 158

Chapter 39. Day 18. Broome to Cape Keraudren. 166

Chapter 40. Day 19. Cape Keraudren to Wickham. 178

Chapter 41. Day 20. Wickham to Carnarvon. 182

Chapter 42. Day 21. Carnarvon to Dongara..................................184

Chapter 43. Day 22. Dongara to Perth. 189

Epilogue. 192

A note to the reader:

I wrote "Diamonds on the Road" in 2005 to refresh my memories of my experiences of motorcycling in northern Western Australia, with two of my sons watching over me from a Range Rover. When I wrote it I had no intention of publishing what I then regarded as a personal memorandum of my thoughts and experiences of the trip.

Then I wrote and published "Egotecture" – a resumé of an architectural tour of parts of Europe – and later "Issues and Challenges" – my idiosyncratic views on matters I consider need thoughtful and balanced discussion.

Now, having been advised by my literary son Nicholas, I have published "Diamonds on the Road". I hope readers will find my memories of an earlier world, and my thoughts during my ride, of interest.

Chapter 1.
On the Road Again.

Human beings are ridiculously complicated creatures. I cannot understand them and I have found that the older I get and the more experienced I become the less, not the more, I understand them and their motives. Why have we humans followed such terrible leaders as Adolph Hitler, Joseph Stalin, Genghis Khan or Pol Pot?

How do we arrive at the conclusions we arrive at? Why are there devoted communists and devoted conservatives? Why are some of the activities in which we involve ourselves regarded as trials and we try to dodge them and why are other activities regarded as enjoyable? These are constant puzzles.

Why is bouncing around in a small boat getting sunburned and dangling a line on the end of which is a dead whitebait impaled on a hook, with the object of enticing a poor unsuspecting fish to a painful death, a pleasure and sitting in front of a computer in air conditioned luxury creating a technical drawing work, and therefore not enjoyable? Why is being confined to a small cabin on a huge, crowded ship a desirable adventure? How does the human race decide such things? Why is hitting a small round white object along a tree lined green sward with a bent stick with the object of getting it into a small hole a joy but trimming hedges a chore and a bore?

Why have I enjoyed riding my motorcycles over many of the roads of Australia and some of the roads of the Middle East in weather ranging from cold, wet and miserable to steamy and uncomfortably hot when I could have seen the same countryside in air conditioned luxury on four wheels? These are questions I must ponder further. Perhaps I will find answers. Perhaps not.

The following pages contain some reminiscences and a wander through my thought patterns during a motor cycle ride from Perth to Kununurra and back in 2005.

Born, as I was, in 1932 the ride was, almost certainly, my last long ride. I have added a bit of background on my life as a motorcyclist, some short tales from previous journeys, anecdotes about people that have influenced me for good or ill, some recent history and some of the thoughts that come into the mind of a long distance rider.

Although the story is centred round the journey, as with any long distance ride there are diversions and meanderings so it is not simply a travel story. Long distance motor cycling is a solitary pursuit. Trapped for hours inside a helmet, sitting in a more or less fixed position, gives the mind a chance to wander onto its own byways. Its "inward eye that is the bliss of solitude" (Wordsworth) swings into action. Ordinary things are seen with different eyes and diamonds of thought well up, usually unbidden.

Chapter 2.
Why This Book?

I suppose all those who write wonder why they do so. What motivates me to now write about the motorcycling part of my life and what is probably my last long ride over an interesting section of Western Australia? I have not reached any reasonable conclusions.

I know that making the effort will give me the chance to relive the experiences of the ride but is that a good enough reason for sitting for hours in front of a keyboard?

Part of me wants to share the joys and sorrows of long distance riding with others who have not had the urge to try it or have not had the opportunity. To give them some inkling of what it is all about – a taste of what it is like to tear through the buffeting air on two wheels. Maybe those who also have enjoyed long distance motorcycling will identify with my story.

The other part of me rejects the discipline of sitting for hours at a keyboard. The only solid conclusion I have reached is that although some might find some interest in my ramblings it is unlikely that a large audience will find them enthralling and some of the thoughts I have had as I rode along, which are reported in this, are almost certain to irritate many of those who read them. So entertaining the masses does not appear to be my motive and I know that sitting and pecking at a keyboard with my two forefingers for long periods is not going to entertain me – so I ask again - why?

Others write for financial reward, to leave their mark on the literary canon or to record notable events. None of these apply in this case. So although I have not so far found any sound reason for writing anything at all I am going to doggedly continue with my story of motorcycling and of the trip.

Maybe I will uncover reasons for writing it as I go along in the same way I have found reasons for journeying as I have gone along on my rides. Perhaps some of my family and friends will struggle through this slim book out of a sense of duty and as it contains photographs of the magnificent scenery of the west of the Australian continent and its unique flora, and fauna those who appreciate her beauties should find a degree of interest.

Those with a low boredom threshold or who want excitement in their reading, into whose hands this falls, are advised to proceed no further.

*Young Peter aboard the side valve Matchless. Note the right hand gear change.
This was taken in 1933 or 1934. It was accurately coloured by my father but age has faded it.*

Chapter 3.
My Early Motorcycling Background.

I have ridden on motorcycles since I was an infant. My father had a 1000cc, side valve, V twin Matchless when I was born. He was still riding it when he was killed in an industrial accident when I was 22. Although I do not remember the experience I believe I was transported around on it as an infant wedged between my parent's bodies.

Dad later attached a sidecar to his solo machine to transport my mother, my younger sister and me in more comfort. I still remember the joys of tearing along in the sidecar when quite small and going as far afield as my aunt's farm outside the wheat belt town of Corrigin.

When I was a little older I used to sit on the machine parked in its garage at 234 Canning Highway, South Perth, twist the throttle and make growling noises that were supposed to represent engine noises. Later still I learnt to ride on it with its sidecar still attached.

After Dad was killed, and when I was in a very depressed state, I let someone take the Matchless and its sidecar away. I have no idea what happened to it but I dearly wish I had kept and restored it.

Dad on an earlier Matchless negotiating a bit of poor road. Obviously obstacles did not daunt him.

Chapter 4.
My Dad and Further Motorcycling Background.

My small, tough and determined Dad used his solid framed, cast iron engined motor cycles to tour the south west when, with the terrible roads and the lack of facilities of the time being what they were, that was an heroic thing to do. Looking back I am astounded that he managed to get the heavy and unforgiving, two wheeled road graders to the places he took them. With its right hand gear lever and left hand clutch Dad was obliged to let go of the handlebar and the throttle of the V twin with his right hand when he changed gear. This would have been an adventure on those badly corrugated roads.

Dad was a wiry and adventurous man with brown eyes and dark curly hair. He was slightly under what was then average height. He was self contained and shy – especially, when he was younger - with women. He was brought to Australia from Switzerland by his mother when he was very young. Whenever I think of him a line from "Banjo" Paterson's "Man from Snowy River" comes to mind. "He was small, and tough and wiry, just the sort that won't say die".

My grandmother was a lady of strong character who believed in honesty, honour and hard work and brought up her eight children, and later my sister and me, strictly. Like many Swiss she was serious and she sometimes acted as though humour was a frivolity that had little place in her orbit.

Early in the 1900s Australia needed such hard working people and she and her husband, Walter Bruechle a mining engineer, played their part in the mines of Zeehan, Tasmania, and in the goldfields at Kalgoorlie and Coolgardie. My father was my grandmother's first child. She and Walter produced another seven children, Vera, Walter, Theresa, Elsa, Maja, Conrad and Erica, in Australia. So my father was the eldest of the brood.

What I am now going to relate is family lore picked up by the large ears of a small boy. Forgive me if it is not completely accurate historically. In the early 1900s when Dad was young the family lived in the Goldfields of Western

The young Johannes (Hans). This was probably taken during a stint clearing the land for future farming in the Manjimup area that he did.

Australia and he, with his younger brother Wally in tow, explored the bush around the town of Kalgoorlie. They met people such as "Bumblefoot Paddy" an Aborigine who, to keep up with the tribe as they wandered, wrapped a badly broken leg around a sapling and kept up. The sapling became part of his skeleton forever after. Dad and young Wally learnt to be tough and they admired toughness.

Walter Bruechle senior had an accident with a detonator which damaged him and he later developed consumption and was moved to the conservatorium that was then at Wooroloo. I would like to provide more detail about him but I know no more about Walter senior. He was long gone before I was old enough to recognise anyone. His death left my father as the male head of the family.

Dad had an outstanding scholastic record as a young student but with his father's incapacity it was necessary that he find paid work at a fairly early age, so his opportunities in the academic sphere were curtailed. He became an electrician and he continued to practice as one until he was killed at Bunbury.

Australian Blue Metals were opening up a stone quarry and Dad was their leading electrical engineer. He was up a fabricated steel pylon adjusting the main power line into the site when welding gave way, the pylon broke and Dad fell several metres to the ground and broke his neck. I raced down to Bunbury on my Thunderbird Triumph but I was too late. He had died. I was devastated.

Dad also lectured to apprentices at Perth Technical College in the electrical trades department of which his youngest brother Con' was then the head.

I know he went contract clearing in the Manjimup area when he was in his late teens or early twenties, where he met and photographed those who were then involved in a Group Settlement Scheme in the area and he formed a lasting regard for the people and the Karri forest. He made friends with pioneers in the area such as George Starkey, "Tiger" Felstead and Freddy Buckland; friendships that he retained for the rest of his life.

I am unsure when he bought his first motorcycle but I do know that he used it to visit his father at Wooroloo. He joined the Coastal Motorcycle Club and took part in their social events and competitions but his real love appears to have been solitarily roaming the south west.

On one trip he discovered the Stirling Ranges, which was the start of a life

A human pyramid with Dad on top during a Coastal Motorcycle Club club run.

long love affair. He climbed them many times and photographed them. Later he took my sister and me camping in the Stirlings. We spent several Easters under canvas while rain teemed down and, in the rain, climbed some of the lesser hills such as Youngermere.

We had the, now unbelievable, privilege of being alone in Chester Pass all over one Easter break. In my short pants with my bare legs I came to the conclusion that every leaf on every plant in the Stirlings had a hook on it. Our trips were not noted for their comfort but they were exciting.

I continued to visit the mountains for the rest of my life and I took my children there. My last climb was with my youngest son, Hans junior, when I was 69. We climbed Toolbrunup together late in the afternoon and stood on the mountain's crest as the sun set. Vivid reds and the palest of golden blues turned slowly into pale pinks and greys and then into enveloping gloom as the sun disappeared. Magical and unforgettable. Climbing back down in the dark had its hazards though.

Dad met my mother through motorcycling. Her father was a well known speedway sidecar competitor when the racing was at the WACA ground. They

Dad proving he had little fear of the heights in the Stirling Ranges on one of his many visits to them.

married at the height of the depression and produced two children; my sister Paula, some 20 months younger than me, and me, the eldest grandchild.

There were difficulties with the marriage that I vaguely remember though I was quite young. There was a fair age difference between my parents. My mother was never considered to be good enough for her eldest son by my stern grandmother and there were quite marked differences in their temperaments.

There were arguments, probably fuelled in part by a shortage of money during the depression years, so my mother took my sister and left my father and me. He and I lived together in South Perth for a few years where I started school. He was helped out in looking after me by various of my aunts.

It was a time of new experiences for me. Apart from school and learning how the human species interacts I was free to wander after school until Dad came home when there was just the two of us.

One day the "Queen Elisabeth", then the world's biggest and best ship, came and anchored in Gage Roads. Although I was only about 6 I wanted to see it so I set off down Canning Highway to walk to Fremantle. A passing car picked me up and the family in it took me with them as they were engaged on a similar quest to mine. I have no idea who they were but they were obviously wealthy. Only the wealthy had cars in 1938.

They not only transported me to the shore at North Fremantle, they also bought a ticket for me in a small boat that did a circuit of the magnificent hulk, and they transported me back to 234 Canning Highway.

I got home well after dark. I was a bit nervous but I found a parent who was so relieved that I had turned up unscathed he did not carry the matter any further than to tell me not to do anything so foolish ever again – and I have not gone to look at a ship since (well only once or twice).

After two or three years my sister returned and we lived at different locations, one location was North Beach when it was miles from anywhere. Finally we settled in Welshpool, in the old family residence, with my grandmother, after our parents divorced. My mother married again and had a long and happy relationship with her second husband, the two children they produced and their grandchildren.

During the Second World War Dad decided he would like to join the army and see the world. The government would not let him, both because he was too old as he was then in his late thirties, and, more importantly, because he was needed in Australia. He was "manpowered".

Wooden hulled boats, called Fairmiles, were being built near the western end of the Causeway to be used as submarine chasers, and he had the task of fitting them out with their power and communications cabling. The theory was that wooden hulls would not be detected by submarines using the magnetic detection systems of the time.

I was lucky enough to go on an inaugural sail on one down the Swan River when I was about ten or eleven. After the war a couple of the boats Dad had wired were used for the Rottnest run. My scruffy mates and I sailed to the island many times on the "Islander", a converted Fairmile, and the "Wandoo", another boat wired by Dad, doing our level best to drink the bar dry during "34 glass crossings".

In about 1941 Dad bought a 1938 Ford V8. He used it to take Paula and me to different parts of the state after the war ended. During the war years petrol was rationed so the V8 did not get used much but once peace broke out and petrol became more readily available Dad took us to the Stirling Ranges, down to Albany where we camped at Little Grove and even up to Hamelin Bay and the Peron Peninsula, where his old friend George Starkey lived on his own as the "linesman" maintaining the overland telegraph line between Hamelin Pool and Carnarvon. George's *bete noire* were camels who rubbed their itches on his slender steel poles until they pushed them over.

We often went south to Manjimup where Dad's brother Wally had a farm by then. Using Wally's farm as a base we camped near the Warren and Donnelly Rivers, where Dad and Rex Hall fished for trout. Rex was a retired Colonel from India who had left when the "troubles" started, bringing his exotic and pukka presence and accent, his family and the skins of the tigers he had shot to Perth.

It was Rex who, when stopped at a road block on the Causeway by a policeman who suggested he had over imbibed, said, "You know, I think I have finally met Sherlock Holmes".

We camped, caught marron using running snares made from curtain wire, and motored down to the Donnelly Bar using a little Seagull outboard motor Dad had bought and a heavy timber dinghy Freddy Buckland had made.

Looking back I realize how fortunate I have been to have him as a parent. He was patient, hard working and reserved. He encouraged me in many ways. It was with his encouragement that I rode my "Aussie" bicycle, laden down with pots, pans, a sleeping bag and a tent, around the south west of the state for a week with my mate Jim Stephen on his similarly laden "Malvern Star" during the August holidays when we were sixteen.

A little later, after I had learnt the arts of pulling in clutches, twisting throttles and changing gears on the Matchless, together with a kid named Ernie Smith, who lived up the hill in Welshpool, I bought a broken down Chater Lea. It cost £5. We rode it up and down Ewing Street hill. It had no clutch because the motivating lever had fallen off, so it was started by putting it in second gear and then both Ernie and I running madly alongside it until it fired then one or the other would leap aboard as soon as it took off.

Because it had no clutch gear changing was not to be undertaken lightly and stopping required finding neutral, not a task for amateurs, or stalling the single cylinder engine.

The Sturmey Archer gear box withstood a terrible pounding. Later I made a new lever at metal work and we could then de-clutch, but somehow it was not as exciting. I think the neighbours were not as happy about the Chater Lea, which had long lost its exhaust baffles, as Ernie and I were.

Chapter 5.
Ewing Street, Welshpool
and the United Nations at QPSS.

At this stage of my life I do not see myself as anything other than a person of the present. I do not feel that I am of another time – merely experienced. Because I feel like that, even though my body will not now sometimes do the things I have become used to expecting of it, it seems strange to me that others brought up in different circumstances or during a later period might not understand life as I knew it when I was young.

As others do not have the experience of Welshpool as it was, I will now endeavour to redress this sad black spot in their lives to some degree by giving to you (trumpet blast please maestro) – Ewing Street and our home in it. An acquaintance of mine - a well-known architect and son of a well-known architect – named Geoffrey, made me realise that may be the world around did not have the slightest idea of life there when he recently said to me "Goodness! I did not realise that people actually lived in Welshpool".

When I lived there, between the ages of nine and nineteen, (or 1941 to 1951) Ewing Street was a short street that stretched from Welshpool Road to Railway Parade. About one third of its length from Welshpool Road and half way up its gentle slope it had a bend and we lived in a house on a large block just within the bend.

The house was a little, weatherboard place of four rooms – two dressing rooms, a living/dining room and a kitchen – surrounded on three sides by verandah. The four of us, grandmother, father, sister Paula and I slept on beds, covered in winter by heavy blankets knitted out of carefully cut up old stockings by grandmother, on the front and side verandas.

Privacy from the outside world was provided by a timber dado wall above which were large, timber framed asbestos shutters that swivelled to allow in the cooling breezes on summer evenings and closed to keep out at least some of the freezing winds of winter.

At one end of the back veranda there was a small enclosed room with an end window, which served as a playroom for Paula and me and at the other a bathroom in which was an enamel hand basin on a butter box, a galvanised iron, painted bath (eau de nil) and a chip bath heater, also painted a pleasing shade of eau de nil, that supplied hot water. The bath was used only once a week, before we all trooped off to the "pictures" on a Saturday night, and it was shared. Hot water was at a premium and involved feeding the bath heater with small pieces of wood and watching carefully that it did not overheat. Daily ablutions were carried out using the enamel basin filled with cold or, at best, tepid water.

The floor of the house was timber boarding and joists supported on timber stumps and although it was near to ground level at the front of the house it was about a metre and a half above ground level at the rear, which meant that there were stairs down to the "wash house".

This facility contained a copper tub built into a brick and mortar stand under which was a fire box so that the water in the "copper" could be heated. It was filled from a tap and it was one of my tasks to empty the soapy water out of it onto the vegetable garden. Alongside the "copper" were a pair of concrete troughs with a "wringer" mounted on the wall that divided the troughs. The whole was ineffectively protected from the weather by a trellis and a honeysuckle hedge. The floor was old bricks.

It was in the wash house that I rigged up my own radio, a "crystal set". It needed an aerial so I strung a copper wire stolen from Dad's workshop from a distant tree to the brick chimney of the "copper". That little exercise taught me a valuable lesson when the tree swayed in a high wind and pulled the chimney over. Dad was philosophical.

Behind the wash house was a mulberry tree and a vegetable garden in which Dad grew kohl rabi and radishes. The soil was poor even though it had been nourished with cow manure that I had pulled in my little two wheeled cart, made by Dad, across the road from the yard of a cow that the Zucals, who lived opposite, kept.

Over the garden stretched the clothes lines with their forked wooden props bought from an itinerant Aborigine and behind it grew a thicket of bamboo that sheltered the dunny from prying eyes. Each week a man came and removed the dunny's pan and its roiling contents and left us with a nice, freshly tarred replacement.

There were many wonders in the back yard. For many years it had a "racehorse" goanna as an inhabitant. He lived under the mulberry tree and although he was very wary I still managed to stand on him one night when wandering down the back to urinate.

I had just been reading H. G. Wells' book "The Island of Dr. Moreau" about a mad vivisectionist who changed animals into humans and then managed to die leaving the hero of the book to watch the animals slowly reverting to their non human state. The humanoid creatures Dr. Moreau had formed from dogs started to look at him with affection but those formed from carnivores started to look on him as lunch, which frightened both him, and me, badly. Being young and impressionable I empathised with his plight so I was in a highly nervous state as I toddled into the dark.

Then it happened. I stood on the goanna. The slither and the movement petrified me. I screamed and leapt. The goanna took off as only racehorse goannas can.

The back yard also had a large paper bark tree in which I slung a hammock I had made out of old chaff bags held together with nails used as skewers to stitch the various parts together, in which I relaxed and dreamt. From the paperbark I collected dried twigs to act as kindling for the kitchen fire and the bath heater. In the hammock I tried my first, hand rolled cigarette made from tobacco stolen from Dad and wrapped in a Rizla cigarette paper. It tasted foul and left me quite dizzy.

I spent many mindless hours bowling a hoop made out of an old bicycle wheel around the yard and breaking world records or kicking a tennis ball through imaginary goals. I also made forts from holes dug into the grey sand

and defended them against imagined invaders. The yard was big and I was its master.

Each year the extensive family of aunts, uncles and any children who lived in the Perth area assembled at grandmother's house on Guy Fawkes' night. For a few weeks previously we collected dried grass and old branches and built quite impressive bonfires. Fireworks, contributed by everyone, went into a wooden butter box and they were set off by the elders and betters in a controlled manner. We children were allowed only Tom Thumbs and Sparklers. The more interesting fireworks such as Catherine Wheels, "Vesuvius's", Roman Candles, Basket Bombs and Sky Rockets were lit in turn by responsible adults and we all stood around and cheered – except for one year.

Uncle Wally, who was then in the army and of whom you will hear more later, had a great deal of trouble lighting one sky rocket in its beer bottle launching pad. The fuse kept going out. Never one to shirk a challenge Wally kept trying until the fuse was extremely short – and then it ignited and immediately took of – straight up the sleeve of Wally's shirt. With great presence of mind Wally shook the buzzing and fuming thing out of his sleeve to avoid being severely burnt when it came time for it to shower out its innards of stars, let alone being scorched by its tail of fizzing rocket propulsion.

It fell straight into the butter box. What followed was a conflagration of different types of fireworks all going of in a chain reaction. It was spectacular but, alas, all too short. We stood around in an anti-climatic frame of mind watching the bonfire die down and then we all grouped under the Lilac tree where the elders and betters consoled themselves with a few beers and we children discussed the excitements of the evening. We were torn between the short time taken by the excitement and the absolute magnificence of the display while it lasted.

Cooking at most houses in the street was carried out on wood stoves. At our house it was normally done on a Metters No.1 but sometimes, for simple meals, grandmother cooked on her small Hecla, electric oven. With the need for wood for cooking and for the copper and the bath heater I, and others in the street like me, spent a fair bit of our young lives chopping wood and collecting chips and brush to start the fires. The Ford V8 was used for bringing wood down from the Darling Range on week ends or "mill ends" were bought from the local wood carter.

The little weather board house was hot in summer and cold in winter but I do not remember that living there was a trial. It was the way things were. Food was rationed during the war and we shivered a good deal as we walked to school in our bare feet in winter and hopped along quickly on the melting tar of the road in summer but the compensations were many. There were areas of untouched bush and swamps to explore, there were gilgies to be caught in a drain on our way home from school, there was bread and dripping to be hungrily devoured when we did arrive home and there was a sense of freedom that is absent in today's close knit and ordered suburbs. We might have been under privileged by today's, probably over catered, standards but we enjoyed it.

What I find to be an interesting thought is that if our residence, or any other residence in Ewing Street, was offered in a brand new state to a family today they would look at the person who proffered it as though he or she was an imbecile.

No refrigerator, just a funny little wooden ice chest with a lining of galvanised iron and a place to put a block of ice in the top? Don't be ridiculous! No en suite – just a weekly bath and daily ablutions carried out in an enamel basin? Who could live like that? No television theatre with six speakers – just a funny, little, crackling, valved, Bakelite radio with the whole family listening to "Dad and Dave", "Martin's Corner", "Mrs 'Obbs" and, if you were very good an occasional episode of "First Light Fraser" or the dramatisation of Georgette Heyer's latest book? Such deprivation! No climate control – just a small electric fan gently stirring the air in summer and the family huddled around a small, electric, radiant heater cooking toes and leaving backs freezing in winter? Tantamount to death by chilblains or pneumonia! It is astounding how much expectations and demands have changed in seventy short years. Are things now better?

My sadly misguided family thought that having a radio of any description was a luxury and that a radiator and a small fan were gifts from a benevolent heaven. My grandmother let us know that our living conditions were much better than they were in the Kalgoorlie days when things were tough and walls were made of burlap. Have we as a society and as a people advanced from the way things were or have we regressed in many ways? Are the people of today as independent and as able as they then were? I never once heard my elders say that matters were so bad that the government should do something about them, as I hear so often now. They expected that improvements were their own responsibility. I hear many now complain that such luxuries as elective surgery and highly expensive drugs that were not then available at any price, are not readily available for all. Others complain about lacks in climate control of classrooms. Without it the little dears cannot learn anything. I have even heard complaints that there is inadequate assistance for those who are too tired to clean up their own living areas, and complaints about roads that are so far removed from the tracks my Dad rode on he would think they were heaven. Apparently they have to be improved or the people using them are likely to kill themselves. Is the price of progress loss of self-reliance - of independence?

The rest of Ewing Street fared much as we did and in some cases not as well. On the Welshpool Road corner, in a galvanised iron shanty that was primarily a workshop lived the Robinsons with their several children. A couple of the boys were my contemporaries.

Next to them on the western side of Ewing Street lived the Gales and their two boys and a girl. The older boy, Colin, and I were classmates. Next came us and, following us, a little tumble down weatherboard house surrounded by a completely uncared for garden in which lived dear old and frail, Mrs Hazel; who occasionally gave Paula and me lollies over the fence. Later, after the dear old lady had died the house was taken over by Jack and Wynne Grieve and their two young daughters.

Still further up the hill lived others in their little timber boxes. I have forgotten some of their names but I remember the retired Mr. Birch and the house with the savage dog that had run up and down the front fence line so often in defence of his property that he had worn a trench.

Because we played cricket together in the middle of Ewing Street I remember the house in which Johnny and Eddie Kelly and their family lived. Towards the top of the hill lived the Firns. Their residence not only housed the Firns family, it also catered for the Farmer girls, Aileen and Jeanie and my mate, Ernie Smith. When Ron Firns came home from the war - he was a Lancaster bomber pilot – it also housed him, his wife and their small child.

Just over the hill lived the Dickinsons with their two sons and then came the little timber Methodist Church. It was in this edifice, consecrated to the Christian God, that Paula and I received background on the Christian religion from Miss Cox who had an afflicted foot and played the organ while we piped "Yes, Jesus loves me. Yes, Jesus loves me. Yes, Jesus loves me. The Bible tells me so".

Ewing Street was full stopped by the road alongside the railway line. On the corner there was a small timber sawmill that employed Ernie and me to clean up on week ends and who allowed us to drive their "crash box", International truck in the yard.

Opposite the saw mill were the offices and works of what my memory tells me was Structural Steel, a BHP offshoot, for that time a fairly large steel fabrication works. Because the Second World War was then at its peak the steelworks worked double shifts so that we could plainly hear the clanging of steel on steel late at night as we lay in our beds on the verandah. Then there was a patch of bush and then the Pantings with their brood. To the north of the Pantings was the Dorigo poultry farm and alongside them the Zucals with their poultry farm. Next, on the opposite side to the bend in the road to us, lived late arrivals – the family of a well known jockey named Herb' Charles. He had the best house in the street and several horses on his property. He also had twin daughters, Valerie and Shirley, in whom I took a good deal of interest even though they were a couple of years older than I was. Even skinny, little sixteen year olds can dream.

You might now have leapt to the conclusion that Ewing Street was primitive but you would be wrong in many ways. It had those modern marvels, reticulated power and water. The Dorigos had the one telephone in the street but at least there was a telephone so that I could let the folks know I was alright after they let me out of hospital after a motorcycle crash at the bottom of William Street. And there was mutual respect by all those who lived in the street for all others which resulted in a harmony. No one broke into the property of others. There were no late night drunken fights and property destruction. People often helped each other. Dad, being the proud possessor of his Ford V8, was often called on to act as a taxi in an emergency and did so more than willingly.

There were, of course, squabbles among the children but the adults would not dream of attacking each other over them or over anything else. It was quite civilised compared to many areas today. Prosperity and abundance, ready access to alcohol and entertainment through television and housing provided by government has not universally resulted in good manners.

Around the corner in Welshpool Road lived the Hurleys and the Tilbys and then, next door to them, there was a little timber framed hall painted a dull orange, with its walls stabilised by angled timber props. This served as a junior school for the children of the area during the day, with all three years being taught by one teacher, Miss Brady.

It also was used on Wednesday nights by the local youth club where we played table tennis, quoits and darts and on Friday nights as a cinema. Mick Tilby ran the projector and cooked saveloys in a copper outside the hall on picture nights and we, who were lucky enough to be able to afford one at sixpence each, stood around eating them in the steaming cold at half time, drowned, as they were, in tomato sauce and enclosed in a soggy bun. It goes without saying that they were delicious.

Mick and George Milne went on to create the "Bright Spot" chain of fast food outlets, an old time McDonalds and Perth's first such string of outlets providing hamburgers to passers by from caravans, built by the father of the Robinson herd, at strategic spots around Perth and at the Claremont Speedway, and they both finished up driving Rolls Royces.

I think they were only superseded by the caravan of the famous Bernie's on Mounts Bay Road. As a teenager I sold ginger beer from a keg and cooked hamburgers for them on Friday nights at the Claremont Speedway. Because I was there every Friday night I got to know the form of the speedway bike riders. One night a slightly inebriated gentleman asked me if the rider in yellow would beat the rider in green – and I told him "no". He kept coming back for my opinions through the night and at the conclusion of the evening he gave me 5 pounds. It turned out he was betting with his mates and my tips had been pretty good. 5 pounds! 5 pounds! It was a fortune. I was being paid 25 shillings a night.

Next door to the school hall was a shed, that has now been replaced by a highway, that was part of the centre of social and commercial activity in Welshpool – Milne's Store. It was here that the rationed butter, sugar and tea were purchased - and Dad's rationed cigarettes. "Milnes" sold everything including stock and chicken feed. The concrete silos that George Darjeerling

Milne built after the war, when he returned from his stint in the army and as business increased, are still there beside the highway.

Each morning the working men of the area headed off on their stately bicycles with their lunch boxes on their handlebars, walked down to the train station or, as in Dad's case, started their vehicles and went to work. Starting the V twin Matchless with its weak magneto spark was an art form. Much coaxing and many depressions of the kick starter were needed on cold mornings.

We children who had outgrown the local junior school would head down Welshpool Road to our seat of learning - Queen's Park State School - in our bare feet.

If we were lucky we would time our journey to coincide with the run home of Stan Smith, the milkman, in his cart towed by a tiring horse after he had delivered milk to the district. We would jog behind the cart and, occasionally, he would ask one of us if we would like a lift. The privileged one would stand on the tail board of the cart alongside Mr. Smith looking down at the panting, envious followers and smirking.

At school we were given lessons by teachers who tried hard with our motley bunch. The headmaster was an Englishman who had not been out from the Old Dart for very long and who rejoiced in the name of Mr. Bumstead. He inevitably became "Dagwood". He often told us that he had ridden a bicycle from Land's End to John O'Groats as a young man. He taught a bunch of 12 year olds verging on puberty, known then as sixth standard.

The student body was interesting. Most of us were first generation, Australian born children of migrants but there were a number of students who were descended from the inhabitants of our great continent when it was invaded by the Europeans. You see the school was next door to Sister Kate's Home in which was housed what has since turned out to be "the stolen generation". They tended to keep to themselves. The only one of Sister Kate's denizens in my class was Gerry Warber who was noted for his fair skin and blond hair.

There were a number of Greek kids – Nick and Con Psaltis, Micky and Nicky Lucas, Frankie Buttergeig, Manuel Manolas, Manuel Cjuglas, Pauly Paul, Arthur Athaneroff and their sisters and cousins.

Then there were the Pom offspring – Colin Shalders, Bill Mc Neill, Ray Beard, Bob, Don and Harry Robinson, the Sawyers, the Williams, Alf, Fred and Harold Panting, Bruce "Squeaker" Doyle, the Smallhorns, the Comleys, the Allsops and Basil and Florence Humble come to mind.

The three Gales were a Welsh minority and the Scots were represented by Donald and Margaret McDonald. There was even an exotic in Sonny Sher Ali. Where his family came from and why they came to Australia I have no idea.

Then there was me – the solitary male Kraut, when the Krauts were the enemy. We were at war with the Axis powers led by the abhorrent Adolph Hitler and his fellow, much maligned, criminal gang together with swaggering Benito Mussolini (does Berlusconi remind you of anyone?) and the Emperor Hirohito.

We were all part of the war effort. Grandmother knitted socks for the soldiers, Dad built an air raid shelter under the fig tree in the back yard and we older boys dug slit trenches in the school grounds into which we children could all troop in the event of a Japanese air raid.

Boys being boys there was a fair bit of pushing and shoving. We mauled each other in cock fights in which Con Psaltis acted as my horse. We played "Red Rover – All Over" in which one unfortunate stood in the middle of the square of grey sand that was our play area and then the rest of us rushed across from one line to another. The man in the middle had to bring one of the rushers to a halt. Then there were two men in the middle and this went on till there was only one rusher left. I did quite well at that game being small and slippery with a good sense of balance.

We also played "Brandy" in which one kid, armed with a tennis ball, would attempt to brand one of the crowd with it. Once he had done that there were then two. They were not allowed to run with the ball but they could throw it from one to the other. The winner was the last person left unbranded. At that game, being small, I also did quite well.

However when it came to formal games like cricket and soccer I was one of the last picked. My ball skills were limited and the cricket ball hurt me wherever it happened to get to me.

At quite an early age I decided that my calling was devoted cowardice. There was, of course, some bullying. Because I was the smallest kid in the class and because I had the unfortunate habit of sniggering whenever one of my classmates made a hash of an answer in class I was often subjected to retribution. I found the pain of my being bullied could be relieved to a degree by bullying those younger than I was. Ah, happy school days! All character building stuff. There might not have been any political correctness at QPSS but there was also not much real nastiness.

In the class we sat side by side, two to a desk. We did our level best not to learn anything but our best was not good enough and Dagwood forced crumbs of knowledge into our tiny heads despite our efforts. Out in the playground we insulted each other. Words such as Dagos, Poms, Abos and Krauts were flung about but at heart we respected and liked each other. I am not sure that the current spate of political correctness helps with respect or with our liking of each other.

What, you are asking, is the point of this ramble down memory lane? The point is that many of us lived in what would now be called third world conditions, although the houses I visited were always clean and well kept, we went to school barefoot in both summer and winter and we hacked at each other both mentally and physically.

We sat in ice cold and hot classrooms, we had virtually no equipment except for blackboards and chalk and our desks were uncomfortable. Out of this mix, a mix that would cause a modern educationalist to shudder, came some pretty good citizens.

As examples, the Psaltis boys moved from market gardening to marketing vegetables in a big way. Nick's son, Arthur, now runs a successful engineering practice. Nicky Lucas became an Australian cycling champion. Don MacDonald became dux of Perth Boys High School. Not one criminal was produced by my year at QPSS and it even produced an engineer who has been asked to speak at international symposia – me.

May be we need more third world conditions, more teachers like Dagwood who are more dedicated to their calling than to their personal advancement and more challenges to succeed academically.

Nowadays failure academically is not allowed. Fortunately this rather silly state of affairs has not yet permeated the sporting arena or our spectator sports would be all played ineptly by ill coordinated no-hopers with slow reactions.

Although we now, no longer, demand effort from those learning in our public school system that disease has not spread into the sporting arena and sporting types are expected to work hard at achieving excellence and are expected to practice until it hurts. We need to demand more of our young in our educational system, less pandering to the lowest common denominator, less political correctness and less silly theories such as outcomes based education. We should encourage excellence in learning and more effort. Learning is not easy. It takes dedication, discipline, effort and time.

Was Welshpool a good place to live? I think it was.

The family relaxing at Ewing Street.

Chapter 6.
Growing Up.

When I was about 18, with Dad's help I bought a 1936, 500cc, OHV V twin BSA from "Ali" Barber, an older fellow student and a returned serviceman, for £50. Dad and I set about "doing it up". It was pulled down and the engine parts put into a galvanized iron wash tub. "Cord" piston rings were installed to help stifle the engine's habit of ingesting oil and spewing out smoke. Copper petrol leads that had crystallized with the vibrations over the 14 years of its life were annealed and the fixings to the lines re-soldered.

Alan Abbott, a sign writer friend of Dad's, repainted the tank and the frame was carefully sprayed black. Dad defrayed part of the cost and I worked as a grocer's delivery boy to help pay for some of the bits and pieces necessary.

After the bike was back on the road the next trick was to obtain a license to ride it on public highways. This involved getting a temporary license and reading a book on where motorcycles, which were justifiably regarded as noisy beasts at a time before technology silenced their wonderful bellowings, were not allowed to venture after 11 pm in case they disturbed hospitals.

Once the no go zones and the rules of the road had been absorbed aspiring motor cyclists had to front up to the traffic office in James Street, about where the Art Gallery now is, on their bikes with their temporary licenses in their hands.

Some poor motorcycle cop there asked you some questions from the book and set you a route around the city that you were obliged to follow with him in tow on his Harley Davidson to make sure you did nothing too untoward such as not stopping at intersections when the "pointsman" held his hand up against you.

Fortunately there were two of us and the other fellow trying for his license was even more nervous than I. As the three of us came down the ramp at the southern end of the Horseshoe Bridge the cop on point duty saw our entourage coming so he smartly executed a halt manoeuvre. The young bloke alongside me stopped very quickly and then slowly fell over to one side. After he had picked the model up and the pointsman had given us the "go" signal by waving his arm at us we proceeded along Wellington Street, turned right at Barrack Street, turned right again at the Terrace and then back to base in James Street along William Street.

When we arrived at the station there were a string of lovely, shiny Police Harley Davidsons all angle parked in a neat line on the side of the road on their side stands and close to each other. The other contender for a license manoeuvred his machine next in line and then fell over again out of sheer nervousness. This caused a chain reaction of falling Harleys. The exasperated examiner quickly signed my form giving me a pass and as I ducked into the station to get an official, snow white license he proceeded to explain things to my poor mate and to pick up the Harleys. Without such an inept fellow aspirant for a license I might not have been so readily given a pass but alongside him even I looked pretty good.

About this time my grandmother had had enough of dealing with rebellious teenagers. She was aging and beginning to be in need of nurturing herself so Dad, Paula and I left Welshpool and moved into a house in East Victoria Park. My grandmother moved in with two of my aunts.

Looking back I now realize that my father was probably lonely. I was not much help. After we moved I was deeply involved in learning to be an engineer and was almost completely self absorbed, as the young normally are. When I graduated I was even less company because I had discovered the good life so that when I was not at work I was at Rottnest with rowdy friends or playing the games of youth.

During this period Dad was working for Australian Blue Metal, the quarrying group who developed the quarry in the Darling Scarp near Gosnells which still supplies much of Perth's aggregate. Each day he set out on the Matchless for Gosnells at an early hour and returned to a cold house each afternoon.

Paula was also working her way through the trials of youth and Teacher's Training College so she was not much better company than I. It must have been a difficult period for him watching his children, to whom he had devoted so much of his life, drifting away. Then tragedy struck.

ABM was starting a new quarry outside Bunbury and he went down to supervise the electrics. He was overseeing the new, main, overhead power line into the site which was intended to be the supply for the quarry when problems arose.

I am not sure why he did it but he decided that he had to climb one of the pylons supporting the main aerials to make sure all was as it should have been. He was over 50 years old at the time. He successfully climbed the pylon but it broke and he fell to the ground and broke his neck. My Dad was lost to his family forever.

He was a man of talent and dedication. Had he had the opportunities he provided me his life would have been easier and happier. He and his generation left my generation better off for amenities, health and wealth. I know most of my generation have tried to do the same but I see signs everywhere that we have not succeeded in our endeavours as they succeeded in theirs.

Chapter 7.
The Wheat Belt.

In November of 1951, on my refurbished V twin BSA and with my new license tucked into my jacket I rode to Nornakin, a railway siding outside Corrigin, which had a weighbridge and a wheat bin. I had just finished my second year of engineering and my father still had a couple of years to live.

In the early 1950s there were many sidings so that the "Cockies" did not have far to carry their harvest. Most of the wheat was carried on flat top trucks in hessian bags. Hoppers and screw conveyors were in their infancy. At Nornakin I was to live in the weighbridge and weigh wheat trucks over the Christmas vacation break.

I still vividly remember the two punctured tubes I had on the way that I had to patch and the 38 miles that I had to ride down the "rabbit proof fence" on a diabolical road of king sized corrugations on my solid framed BSA. That stretch took me one and a half hours and I went as fast as I could. When I had completed the stretch I ached in every joint and my back still twinges at the thought of the torture.

That part of the ride also saw the demise of my electrical system which shook itself into a state in which it no longer functioned. At Nornakin the "bin attendant" (I was the "weighbridge officer") was already in residence. He was a newly arrived Pom' named Arthur Stevenson.

Arthur and I lived at the siding for several weeks in what used to be described as "blackfeller" conditions until that expression became completely, politically unacceptable. At the weighbridge I weighed wheat trucks both on the way in and on the way out to ascertain how much wheat had been deposited.

Our supervisor, an old friend of my father's named Lance Ainsworth, taught us about farmer's dogs that sat on the running boards of the trucks when they were weighed in then ran around as the trucks were weighed out. This could have resulted in another half bag of wheat being credited to the deserving farmer if we had not been warned of the scheme by the experienced Lance. The standard subtraction was 1cwt (approximately 50kg) per dog.

Arthur and I helped the good blokes, and there was a great preponderance of these, discharge their bagged loads into the wheat bin using a contraption called an "elevator", which was a diesel engined bucket loader with a chute at the bottom into which we emptied the wheat from early in the morning until sundown. The wheat discharged at the top through a pipe into the bin.

In our time off we shot rabbits for stews using my Savage .22 rifle, and showered under a bucket attached to a beam spanning between the bin and the water tank. Incidentally I cannot recommend tank water from bin roofs, flavoured, as it is, with rotting wheat dust and parrot droppings.

We prepared our stews in Arthur's cast iron pot over a mallee root fire. There was no cooling other than a damp cloth over the butter so what was cooked had to be eaten. We slept in sleeping bags on camp stretchers under the stars. Looking back from the lofty heights of today's many comforts it might appear to be awful but, you know, we thoroughly enjoyed it all – and we considered ourselves lucky to be so well paid.

On several Saturdays we rode into Corrigin late in the afternoon for a beer and to go to the pictures and, because my headlight was not functioning, rode back to Nornakin over a badly graded, loose gravel road riding in the headlights of following cars after the pictures ended.

This was a hazardous undertaking as the track between Nornakin and Corrigin not only had sections of loose gravel, it was also equipped with many bends and protruding rocks that the grader could not dent and in part it was possessed of world class corrugations.

You have not experienced real fear until you have had to plunge into utter blackness at 50mph (80kph) when you arrive at a bend and the car's headlights, which you have been using to pick your path, suddenly decide to illuminate the nearest paddock instead of the road on which you have no alternative but to proceed.

One day I retraced my tyre marks and where we had been was quite remarkable. I would not have been brave enough or foolhardy enough to have ridden there in the daylight.

Both Arthur, and remember he was a fair skinned newly arrived Pom', and I thought that we had great jobs living miles from nowhere and labouring for many hours a day under a blazing sun with no refrigeration and no clean water. The youth of today is much better educated and now knows that we were exploited and were being forced to live in third world conditions. This is only one of the many benefits of today's better education.

I am afraid the long framed, solid rear ended, girder forked BSA was not made for loose and corrugated gravel roads and I fell off several times, once as I rounded the home turn into the siding while Arthur watched. I finished up at the bottom of a railway embankment and had to ride up the railway line, bouncing on the timber sleepers, to get out of the cutting.

Arthur was unimpressed with the stability of the bike and told me that if it looked as though it was going to fall while he was on it he was going to bail out. He was not going to have a red hot motorcycle burning holes in his hide.

He did bail out too. One Saturday afternoon, with Arthur on the pillion the monster started to slide at 50mph, Arthur bailed out. I felt the bump of him leave and then managed to wrestle the bike back under control. I even managed a glance back to see Arthur rolling over and over on the gravel road.

I was fine but Arthur was quite damaged. Then he had to get back on the bike, with a dislocated elbow and a fair bit of gravel rash, so I could take him to the doctor in Corrigin. Dr. "Sniffy" (or was it "Snuffy") Jones had many terse words to say about motor cycles, as medical persons were wont to do. Why they are critical when bikes bring in so much business is beyond me.

The corrugations took their toll on the old BSA. The headlight, at best a half candle power affair that had not functioned since my ride down the "rabbit proof fence", fell off, the battery gave up, which did not matter much because there was no headlight and the ignition was magneto powered, and the back mudguard collapsed onto the back tyre without me noticing and cut a groove into its rubber down to canvas.

At sundown on a few Friday nights, on diabolical roads, I rode the 35 miles from Nornakin down to Stretton where I had been invited to stay at the farm of the Mayor of Corrigin by his son John.

John, an older fellow student who had been in the Air Force during World War II, was doing his course under what was known as the CRTS scheme for returned servicemen. There I held hands with John's younger, and very pretty, sister Helen and sneaked kisses whenever the opportunity arose, shot parrots for their dogs and swam in the dam at Yealering with Helen who was then a glorious 21 year old and a qualified teacher. Magical stuff for a 19 year old.

I cannot describe the euphoria of sitting on a farmhouse veranda as the dark slowly enveloped us with Helen's pretty head, scented with fresh Collinated Foam Shampoo, resting sleepily on my shoulder. For those periods I was a privileged prince.

Before dawn on Monday mornings the golden carriage turned back into a pumpkin and I had to bounce back across the corrugations to Nornakin in time to open up the weighbridge.

After Arthur and I had wound up the bin at Nornakin and I had balanced the books Lance Ainsworth transferred me to Yealering to tidy up there. The weighbridge was in the main street which unfortunately gave me easy access to the pub'. I took to going to the saloon bar at sundown for beers and darts with the locals and staying until they shut the place.

One afternoon Helen came into town to tell me she was leaving for Pingelly where she had been posted as a teacher. We walked over to the pub' for goodbye drinks. To my absolute mortification the barman, who had filled me to the brim the evening before, refused to serve me on the grounds that I was underage and therefore illegal. Helen had to get the drinks – beer for her and lemonade for me. I sat there in my work boots, my stubbies and singlet feeling about four years old. I had been put in my place by a community that had not been impressed by a cocky kid who had been in town about five minutes and had apparently stolen the town belle, who also happened to be the mayor's daughter. Before a fall goeth pride.

The old BSA served me well and it got me back to Perth after riding down from Pingelly very early in the morning, with only two layers of rear tyre canvas between me and destruction. You can guess why I went to Pingelly. It was not the success I had hoped for. Helen was with her older and relatively sophisticated fellow teachers and to them, and in fact, I was a callow youth. She was nice, but distant. Her new life had claimed her.

Suffering from heartbreak I set out at 4am riding by moonlight on kangaroo infested roads because I had to be back in Perth to enrol for my final year early that morning at the latest. There I was ambling along in the cool air under a full moon with the shadows of the trees along the sides of the road creating stripes for me to ride through when to my horror one of the shadows moved.

I dived one way and the kangaroo that had been soaking up warmth from the bitumen, dived the other. Had Skippy decided to jump the way I did they would be still scraping me off the road. During the short weeks at Nornakin and Yealering I had many adventures and met many wonderful characters but they have nothing to do with my last ride to Kununurra so their stories will have to wait for another time.

Chapter 8.
Moving On and Up.

After getting a new rear tyre, fitting a new battery and replacing the headlight I sold the BSA to Arthur for what I had paid for it and with the wealth I had accumulated on the weighbridge I prowled the second hand motorcycle shops until I found a 500cc vertical twin Royal Enfield that appeared to be good value, in a motorcycle showroom on the corner of Roe Street and William Street. I rode that for the last year of my engineering course and for a while after I joined the State Civil Service.

One of my big adventures with the Royal Enfield was to ride it down to my Uncle Norm's farm at Cowaramup one Easter and then to ride back to Collie to catch up with Ron and Lyle, with whom I was planning on watching the motorcycle "round the houses" motor cycle races in Bunbury. Ron had a Velocette and Lyle a Triumph. We tore out of Collie early on the morning of the race and I proceeded to demonstrate the superiority of the Enfield on the winding Collie/Roelands road until it decided to shed its big end bearings just short of Roelands. That night it finished up on a semi trailer with many of the race bikes with me sitting along side it freezing as we returned to Perth.

The Royal Enfield was also involved in one of my less glorious misadventures. On Show Day I picked up Dad from his workplace, Bramley and Dix, near the intersection of Hay Street and George Street. The undertaker Donald J. Chipper was on the corner. I was there to take him home to Welshpool. He had taken his Ford V8 in for servicing at Lynas Motors, which was a short distance away in Hay Street, and the service had not been completed. As we left B&D it was raining, as it always then did on Show Day.

He was not a happy pillion passenger. He insisted that I was going too fast. I explained to him with all the resigned patience a 19 year old could muster that I was the rider and he was the passenger. As we neared home I turned from Swansea Street into Welshpool Road. I carefully gauged the distance to the wet tramlines that then ran down the middle of Welshpool Road and thought with a certain smug satisfaction that my selected "line" would miss them by a good six inches.

I did not see the patch of oil on that line and the next thing I knew I was bouncing down the road with the Enfield in front of me with sparks flying from the metal parts as they ground themselves away on the bitumen road. I jumped to my feet and tore after the beloved motorcycle. After I had hoisted it onto its wheels and found that the damage was superficial I suddenly had a lurching stab of concerned thought. Where was Dad? He was stretched out on the highway resting peacefully between the tramlines. I propped the bike on its stand and ran to Dad who was groaning quietly. We had both lost a fair bit of skin but nothing was broken. He gingerly got back on the pillion and we went home where we salved and bandaged each others wounds. He did not complain once. My eldest son Nick is very much like him.

The Enfield and I had another adventure the night I finished my final examinations. After several days of swotting until 3am and then sitting for the exams I was exhausted. I was also trying to organize the Engineering Students and Graduates dinner for the following night. There I was, near sundown, in fairly heavy traffic heading west on the Enfield in Terrace Drive and about to cross the bottom of William Street, then a two way street. A utility was heading north in William Street, on my left, coming from the direction of the river and Sydney Anderson Motors, the first 24 hour petrol station in Perth with the motto "We never sleep". I was confident he would stop because the rule in those days was that you gave way to the vehicle on your right.

It was misplaced confidence. He did not stop until he was squarely across my bows and only a few feet away. I braked wildly on the tramlines that were there and then the Enfield and I cascaded, face first, into the driver's door of the ute. I came up bleeding from the face and more than a little displaced. I was busily enquiring about the driver's ancestry, the marital state of his parents and his intelligence when a policeman arrived, followed shortly thereafter by an ambulance.

The policeman told me to pipe down, to stop trying to intimidate the poor driver, who was large and Slavic and would have had no trouble dealing with an angry ant like me, and to get into the ambulance. I was too worried about my bent bike and too interested in tearing expletive laden strips off the driver to consider a namby pamby thing like an ambulance. Quite a crowd had gathered when, at the crescendo of my performance and to my horror, I saw a gorgeous girl I had been attempting to talk into going out with me and, still worse, her mum, on the edge of the pavement looking on, with fascinated horror at the bloodied and out of control thing that was me shouting at all and sundry, including the long arm of the law. Although I still wanted, rather badly, to punch the driver and I was worried about my bike I meekly entered the ambulance and was driven to Royal Perth Hospital where they patched up my face and a 50mm deep hole in my leg into which the brake lever had penetrated during the crash.

Next night Shirley was at the Engineering Student's dinner with someone else and I turned up with pieces cut out of my hair, which was a strange shade of green due to the disinfectant that had been used on me rather liberally, fresh, mottled scabs all over the place, and with a slight concussion and a stiff right leg that meant I was a bit wobbly. I had learnt for the first time, but not the last, that motor cycles and romance are a difficult mix.

The Enfield was repaired while I acted as the weighbridge officer at Trayning. The very next time I rode a bike was when I came down to Perth at Christmas. On Christmas Eve Colin Brown and I rode out to see my sister and her friend Joan in Maylands on his Matchless 500cc single and it rained. Colin offered me the front seat and the controls on the way home and I jumped at the chance for a ride. Coming home down Lord Street well after midnight the driver of a parked car threw open the driver's side door just as we approached, I dived out onto the wet tramlines to miss it and the next thing was that the Matchless, Colin and I were all bouncing down the road. By now I was well versed in the instability of two wheels. Colin forgave me.

After I returned from Trayning, where I learnt to play two-up and canasta, where there were wonderful characters with names such as "Porky" and "Jumbo" and where the locals drank large beers called "Sergeant Majors", I looked for a job and was lucky enough to get one with the Architectural Division, Public Works Department.

The Enfield was repaired so I rode it for a while and then I sold it. At age 20 I bought a 650cc Thunderbird Triumph from Don Frearson. It was nearly new. Don had set his heart on a Tiger 110, a bike guaranteed to do 110 miles per hour, and one had turned up so he wanted to unload the Thunderbird that he had only just run in.

The Thunderbird duly had its inlet and exhaust ports polished in John Wearne's garage under the guidance of Harry Gibson who then held the state speed record and with that modification it ran at 114mph, which was an exciting speed on the roads of the time.

As with many of my more prized possessions the Triumph and I had some unhappy experiences. One Friday night, after work, I parked it near the kerb outside the main entrance to the Palace Hotel and trundled down to the bar in the basement – "The Dive" – to have a beer with the young architects and the press gang that then inhabited it. There they all were, "Hawk" Jacobs, Paul Rigby, Ron Saw, "Gus" Ferguson, Brian Jackson, Gene Mapp and even such later luminaries as Bob Juniper, the artist, and John Oldham, the landscape architect and historian.

For some reason I decided to get out early so I wended my way back to the Terrace and there found an old car backing towards my precious machine. I shouted but the car kept coming and the impact pushed the Triumph over onto the kerb and smashed the headlight "nacelle". I was livid. I ran around to the driver's side and screamed at the woman driving. She got out and ran away leaving two small children crying in the rear seat.

After picking the model up I went into the Palace and rang the gendarmes to report the accident so that I could claim insurance. They took a good deal of interest in the matter and sent two burly men in blue around to interview me. They were not very concerned about the Triumph but they were worried about the children. They decided that I was to stand on the corner of St. George's Terrace and William Street while they hid over the road and when the woman came back I was to let them know. They would then deal with the matter.

It seemed to be a sound scheme but as with many sound schemes it turned out to have flaws. She eventually turned up and I approached her. She took one look at me and started heading for parts unknown again. In a fit of madness I grabbed her by the arm. The picture crowd were parading down the Terrace and in the middle of the crowd there I was, hanging on like grim death to the harridan's arm and being battered about the head by a large lady's handbag. I badly wanted to let go but the police had told me to waylay her if I saw her. At that stage a large gentleman came out of the front bar of the Palace – there was a door onto the corner – and offered me physical violence if I did not let her go.

By then I was pretty fed up with being belted around the head with a heavy handbag and the crowd that had gathered were certainly not barracking for me so I did the manly thing and let go. She scuttled back up William Street and I wandered across to the alley that Constables Frame and Gale were inhabiting, on the other side of the Terrace beside the ANZ bank, and told them my sad story. They wanted to be introduced to the large gentleman. I did not want to go much further with the whole matter.

My bike was damaged and the adventure had lost its shine. Half Perth had seen me fighting with a woman and although that might be standard fare these days at that time it was generally thought poorly of. They prevailed, so I wended my way into the front bar and said to the knight in shining armour "Mate – there are a couple of blokes outside that want to see you". He came out behind me full of beer and bluster and ran slap bang into two officers at least as large as he.

I left them to it and plodded back down to the Dive for a nerve settler. Two schooners and I decided I had had enough for the night. When I got back on the Terrace there was Constable Gale in the main doorway of the Palace holding onto the lady's arm and being belted about the head with the same handbag that had given me several bruises. He was made of sterner stuff than me and he hung on and eventually subdued the lady.

Unfortunately he saw me and he told me I had to go to the Police Station and make a statement. The car, the two screaming children and a very reluctant lady was driven off to the Police Station followed by me on a battered motor cycle with a wonky headlight. It was not one of my better Friday nights.

Another night I was riding home at a stately pace east in Shepparton Road,

This was taken on the day that the Thunderbird, with me lying on the tank, head down, feet trailing, to cut down the drag coefficient, ran at 114mph (180kph) on Muchea straight. Note the protective clothing. At least I wore goggles. Also note the headlight "Nacelle". Every time the bike fell or was pushed over I had to get a new one.

at about 5.30pm, when I passed someone on a Norton motorcycle. For some reason he tagged on behind me without me being aware he was there, which did not prove to be a good decision on his part. I turned into Swansea Street to cut across to Welshpool Road and there at a bus stop, just short of Oats Street, was parked a big green Metro bus disgorging passengers. I could not see what was coming in the opposite direction so I braked. This caused the fellow on the Norton to run into me and that bent my rear brake lever up at an angle at which it would only function if depressed 3 inches into the surface of the road. I snatched hard at the front brake and the nipple soldered onto the brake cable pulled off, leaving me brakeless. I dodged out around the Bus and started changing gears to lower ratios to slow down. Thankfully there was nothing coming the other way. When I was going slowly enough I U turned and went back. The Norton and its rider had ducked left around the bus and had mounted the footpath where he cut a swathe through the alighting passengers. Some of the passengers were being fairly critical of motorcyclists but no one was really hurt. The policeman who came to tidy the mess up decided it was not my fault but he told me to get my brakes fixed and to report my side of the proceedings at a police station next day. I went home, straightened out the rear brake rod and double soldered a new nipple onto the front brake cable.

The next night I gave Des Stevenson, a draftsperson of Irish extraction, a lift on the Triumph, after work, from the PWD offices behind the Barracks, where the Freeway now runs, down to the Adelphi, an hotel on the corner of Mill Street and the Terrace where an office building that is attached to the Parmelia now stands. The idea was that I would drop him off, go over to the Police Station to report the accident I had been involved in the night before and then re-join him for a beer.

Des, with his pebble thick glasses that magnified already large eyes, his Royal Irish Rifles background and his jovial, Irish ebullience, was quite a character. He once drank a gallon and a quarter of beer in the front bar of the "Melbourne" during a Friday lunch hour for a bet and then went back to work.

I stopped just short of Mill Street and unloaded Des onto the pavement. There was a "pointsman" on duty controlling the traffic and he saw fit to wave my traffic stream on. Neither he nor I noticed a lone pedestrian staggering over the road through the traffic after a period of relaxation in the Adelphi.

I accelerated hard from the kerb to beat the traffic and suddenly I was presented with a, none too steady, gentleman right in front of me. I leaned left. He jumped forward. I reversed my lean. He jumped back. I straightened up and braked hard. My re-soldered nipple and my rear brake rod all held but I did not stop before I got to him. He fell across my front mudguard, balanced there for a couple of metres as I stopped and then dropped off to one side.

Pandemonium ensued with traffic and gawking bystanders everywhere. The pointsman and I took the somewhat shaken gentleman into the foyer of Shell House which was then on the north side of the Terrace and examined his wounds. They were not too serious so the Cop told me to go and report the accident.

At the Police Station I reported the previous night's Swansea Street fracas and when I had that out of the way I said "And another thing".

The Triumph was a good bike and it carried me down to Bunbury in record time one day. Australian Blue Metal had rung to tell me that Dad had been involved in an accident but that they thought he was going to be alright. I left work with a feeling of dread mixed with optimism and I rode as hard as the Thunderbird would go but I still arrived too late.

My father had died after his industrial accident. I was devastated. Then I had to stiffen my spine, identify Dad's body and be taken by the police to the scene of the accident to see his workmates. Next morning I realised I had responsibilities and I spent the morning arranging for the transport of his body to Perth for his funeral. I rode sadly back to Perth that afternoon. I did not know it then but Wally, one of Dad's two brothers, who had been contacted with the sad news, was trekking up from Manjimup at the same time in a borrowed vehicle, just behind me.

Chapter 9.
Europe and Civilisation.

In 1956, when I was 23, I sold the Thunderbird and went to Europe on the, then mandatory, civilizing tour for young Australian professionals. We took in the wonders of Corb' and Nervi, the Eiffel Tower, the Rome railway station's trend setting cantilever, the beautiful cities of Italy, Switzerland, Germany, France and Austria, and the inspiring Gothic Cathedrals. We lived in bed-sits in Lancaster Gate, Kensington and Earl's Court with gas rings on the floor, on which we cooked our sausages. We went to the National Film Theatre alongside the Thames on grey Sunday afternoons and were smitten by films directed by Eisenstein, Satyajit Ray and Leni Riefenstal. We drank at the Prospect of Whitby, where we sang along with Rolf Harris, and at the Duke of Albemarle, where we talked architecture. We sat around on dim, wintry Sunday afternoons in our bed-sits cooking sausages on our gas rings, smoking cheap Woodbine cigarettes and bemoaning the poor quality of English radio programs. Or we wandered around London by "tube" or on foot in our duffle coats with our hands thrust deeply into our pockets.

I worked for one of London's top engineering consultants, Felix Samuely, who had escaped from Nazi Germany when he saw Hitler's writing on the wall, with clever and dedicated engineers on projects that I found challenging and of huge interest. Samuely was a university friend of the man who taught me the wonders of statics and virtual work, Erich Shilbury.

The projects on which I worked included the American Embassy in Grosvenor Square and the British Exhibition Buildings for the World Fair in Brussels the following year. Willie Frischmann, who had escaped from Hungary as the Russians took over and who was later to design structures for some of London's landmark buildings, and I journeyed down to the National Physics Laboratory at Teddington to get our simultaneous equations solved on a machine the size of a residence that was called the "Electronic Brain". This had a capacity much less than that of any household computer these days. Simon Wolf took me to the Players Theatre in Charing Cross where part of the fun was to put "colonials" in their place. They were heady times. But I digress. This is about motorcycling, not a series of reminiscences of the good old days.

Chapter 10.
Home, Marriage and More Motorcycles.

In March 1957 I flew home to my fiancée, Lynne Jackson, in a Super Constellation when flying was still a rare adventure and the trip took several days. I got on in Rome early in the morning, after a couple of days in the snow of Zurich and Innsbruck, and we flew to a snowy Istanbul for breakfast. That night we landed in Karachi to re-fuel and the following night in Singapore where we stayed at the Raffles, although I spent most of the night exploring what was a completely new and exotic world.

When I fronted up to the counter in Rome to confirm my flight it was found that a mistake had been made with my booking and that I had been seated in the first class section. It was terrible luck but I have learnt to take the bad with the good.

I sat next to an American named Harry Manly. He was a senior pilot with what was then the globe's premier airline - Pan-Am. Harry was flying Qantas because he was charged with flying all international airlines with a view to selecting the best practices of them all. You see he was helping set up Thai Airlines. Because of Harry I got to have a have a shower in the crew's quarters in Karachi and a beer with the air crew while the rest of the passengers sweltered in a tiny lounge that did not have that modern aid to comfort – air conditioning.

In Singapore Harry and I shared a room in that most exotic of hotels, the Raffles. He slept while I charged around a city that I had heard a good deal about from my friends John Wearne, whose father had car agencies there, and Tony Brand my architect friend who had lived there as a boy. I wanted to absorb as much as I could of what was then a completely different world. I was enchanted with the thought that it was possible to get into a strange looking, tubular box with long, slender elements protruding from each side and to get out of it in a completely different place living in a completely different time. This enchantment is no longer possible. Now, wherever you go, there are McDonalds, similar clothing, cars that are the same the world over and a pervasive wish to take as much as possible from rich tourists, unless you really do get into the outback. As I wandered around the marvellous old Singapore I noticed that my stomach hurt. It had for some time. It turned out later that I was nursing a stomach ulcer. Good old helico bacter. Next morning I left Harry behind and headed for Perth, landing in the early evening. The travel adventure was over but the future looked rosy.

Lynne and I married shortly after I returned, started our 25 years of marriage together and started producing our wonderful children. Motor cycles were forgotten.

I returned to the Public Works where I was fortunate enough to be involved in the design of public buildings – schools, hospitals, University buildings and libraries. I worked with Norm' Gilchrist, who later became my partner, in a group of top quality engineers and draftsmen led by the great Lew Harding. The Architectural Division was a marvellous training ground for young architects, engineers and draftspersons and I deeply regret that a later government, under Brian Burke, decided to disband it. It had a proud history from its inception under George Temple Poole up to the time I left when A. E. (Paddy) Clare, a devoted civil servant, was in charge.

My old teacher and mentor, Erich Shilbury, asked me to lecture at night school at Perth Technical College (now Curtin University after having transmogrified from PTC to the Western Australian Institute of Technology to CU) and I also spent time designing structures for young architects who were my friends, as "private jobs", then frowned on by the government for whom I was working.

In 1961 I left my safe job in the Architectural Division and, although Lynne and I then had three children with another on the way and I had, fairly recently, burst a stomach ulcer, started a practice. It was a brave (foolhardy?) move but it was backed by several architect friends, many of whom then supported me throughout my career, and my trusting wife.

For the next few years I spent my time working, drinking at the Celtic Club with the ebullient Irish, being a father and playing golf occasionally, more or less in that order. Life was full and years passed without motorcycles intruding on it.

Then Murray Slavin and Rick Cameron, a couple of recently graduated architects joined my group which had grown and gained partners and staff. They had 350cc, Kawasaki road/trail motorcycles. I took to borrowing one or other of them to run down to the University of WA to give lectures to architectural students. At the same time I was given a couple of commissions to design his factories by Maurie Moller, the founder of Osborne Metal Industries, who rode moto-cross bikes, then called, for good reason, "scramble" bikes. He owned a couple of them – Husqvarnas. He was the patron of a motorcycle club and he was still riding competitively. Together we went up to his home track near Noble Falls where I learnt how to fall off with incredible grace on bumpy corners.

I was hooked again. I bought a second-hand trail bike, a Bultaco Matador, and with Rick, Murray and others I went to such places as the Pinnacles, where we tore around and jumped the bikes over steep sand drifts when that desecration was allowed. My 250cc Matador would not run with their bigger, 350cc Kwakas on the road so I upgraded to a 350 Montadero. This was fine but it had the unfortunate habit of seizing its piston when it became too hot. This locked up the back wheel and led to some hairy moments on corners until the clutch was disengaged.

After a trip back to Perth from Broome, in 1965, via many by-ways such as the 80 Mile Beach, Cape Keraudren, Marble Bar and Whim Creek with Cyril White and Ken Broadhurst in an old Land Rover (another adventure with some wonderful and memorable highlights) I conceived the idea of riding the 80 Mile Beach, but not on the Montadero. I wanted something more reliable.

My wife Lynne, abetted by Rick and Murray traded the Bultaco in on a 4 stroke 350cc XL Honda for my birthday. I rode that around for several years but the 80 Mile Beach trip did not eventuate, due to the pressures of running a practice, and I traded it in on a 250XL Honda for my eldest son, Nick, for his seventeenth birthday.

In about 1978 I had fallen in love with the new, in line 4, DOHC, 900cc Honda, with an appealing name – the Bol D'or. I rang Honda Australia in Sydney and ordered one with panniers attached, then flew across to pick it up. I was 46.

My old mate Derry Barry met me at the airport and we proceeded to partake of some, but not all, of the delights of King's Cross. The upshot of our night on the tiles was that next morning I was out at Blacktown with a thundering hangover to pick up a machine that was considerably bigger and weightier than any I had ridden for a long time. I looked at it and the heavy stillness of dread descended on me. I was not only committed to riding the monster across the continent but more immediately and worse – I was committed to riding it to my hotel in King's Cross in Sydney traffic on a Friday afternoon, I was feeling far from well and I did not know the way.

I was well and truly daunted but with true grit, a strong sense of self preservation, some luck and a surprising display of tolerance by the drivers of Sydney I made it to my hotel. It proved to be the hardest part of the trip.

Chapter 11.
Across Oz on a Motorcycle for the First Time.

Next day I found my way out of Sydney and wandered down through Yass to Canberra where I stayed with an architect friend, the late Bryan Dowling. Despite some early rain it was a great experience and my first taste of distance cycling. Bryan introduced me to Ross Gibson, still a staunch friend. Ross was persuaded by Bryan to give my firm the commission for the structure of an hotel he was to build in Northborne Avenue, the Canberra Motor Inn. Pleasure was combined with work.

A couple of days later saw me nonchalantly sauntering down the Highway to Melbourne where the hotel I normally stayed at when I was in that town turned me down after seeing me cross their threshold in my wet and muddy bike gear. I have not been back since.

The reaction of hotel staff to motorcyclists varies amazingly. I have been looked down on and turned away by some very mediocre establishments and I have been welcomed with interested questions about the bike I was riding from some very up market hotels.

I had lunch next day with an old friend, Allen Pizzey, and set out in the early afternoon along the Geelong road. That night I finished up at Camperdown where I had a riotous night at the local pub' with some really good blokes. I had the feeling that if I had turned up in a three piece suit and a tie in my

Porsche they would not have wanted to know me. Because I was on a bike I was bought beers.

I was getting the hang of distance riding. But that trip is another story. It did whet the taste buds for long distance motorcycling on the great continent of Australia for both Nick and me. Nick rode his little 250 up to Kalgoorlie and we rode the last stretch together. I had enjoyed the experience so much I did it all again four years later.

Young Ben tries the Bol d'Or following my trip. Note panniers at rear.

Chapter 12.
The Motorcycling Environment.

Riding a bike is quite different from driving a car. On a bike you live in the elements and savour, or are revolted by, the smells. You are a part of your surrounds and although the countryside tears past relentlessly you still come to grips with it in a very personal way.

In the air-conditioned splendour of a car, travelling is a bit like watching television. On a bike you know it is hot, cold, wet or dry, windy or still, the air insect laden, dust filled or sweet and soft. Dead animals impose their odour on you. You catch their pungent flavour before you see them. Hot winds buffet you and dry you out.

Then there is the ever present suspicion of danger. You know that you are in unstable equilibrium and that any lack of concentration can bring you down, so you have to be more alert and you feel more alive. Motorcycling has its downsides but there is great satisfaction and interest in riding a road such as the Great Ocean Road in Victoria, the highway through the hills on the way to Mount Isa and the Fitzroy Crossing to Hall's Creek road through spectacular countryside.

The other feature of the motorcycling environment is that you are completely on your own. Even if you ride with a group, and I never have, there is just you and the bike. Sometimes the scenery or the challenges of the road are enough to keep you completely absorbed in what you are doing but on the stretches of the Nullarbor your mind falls in on itself and you ride along pondering matters that would not impose themselves on you in the world of the electronic media or under the stimulation of other people. Those who have not experienced it might be surprised but long distance motorcycling is thought provoking.

The CX 500 Turbo I bought in Sydney and rode across the Nullarbor. It's still in great shape, as this 2019 photo shows.

Chapter 13.
Across Australia Again.

My next ride started in Sydney again, in 1982, this time on a V twin, Turbo charged Honda CX 500. I bought one of the first two imported into Australia. Alan Jones, the Formula 1 champion, bought the other. At the time of writing this I still have mine. This time I had to run up 500km for the first, free service. I did this by travelling north to Kuringai and then heading up into the lower reaches of the Dividing Range.

Just on sunset I found myself at a place called Kurrajong Heights and I stopped at the inn to moisturize a desiccated throat and to check the Test cricket score. It was a mistake. A young bloke asked me if the Turbo was mine and when he found out it was he insisted on buying me a beer. Naturally I had to buy him and his friends one in return and the next thing I knew it was closing time and Sydney was far away and the world had become a hazy, if happy place.

Just getting the Turbo up the gravel hill to the motel units was about all I could manage. They were great blokes who told me hilarious stories of what happened when they went "down" to Sydney, which they seemed to regard as a foreign country. In Sydney they were often forced to "fix up" young city dwellers who picked up their obvious bucolic simplicity and were nasty to them. Next morning I set out early, but not too bright, to have the bike serviced in Blacktown.

I started the main ride by going north to Surfer's Paradise by the coast road. I was looking at a job there with the Hilton Hotel chain and I wanted to see the fabled north eastern part of New South Wales with its many rivers. The Coastal Highway is a great ride but there were hazards and there are also unusual sights. The road was that section of highway on which there were more accidents than on any other stretch of road in Australia, and when they had an accident it was almost always spectacular.

In northern New South Wales and southern Queensland bright green banana palms and grey, green eucalypts rub shoulders. Every kilometre brought new sights and experiences, some of which were not so welcome, such as remarkably poor road surfaces, and some of which were welcome, such as motorists flashing their headlights to warn of speed traps.

It was a Friday afternoon when I arrived at Surfer's Paradise so I dropped in on some fellow consulting engineers I had not seen for a while. It being Friday we drank at their office and one beer led to another.

When I finally turned up at the Hilton the receptionist was unimpressed with my still damp motor cycle gear, my several days of facial growth and the fact that I was breathing beer fumes all about as I sidled up to her desk. In a tone of voice that brooked no argument she informed me that there were no rooms available. I could see my name on her book and pointed it out to her. It came as quite a blow to the poor young lady that I was a guest of the management. I went upstairs, shaved, showered and changed into a sleek, dark blue silk, French, roll neck, long sleeved skivvy and my best dark trousers and re-presented myself. All was forgiven.

After a few days working at Surfer's Paradise I rode south to Canberra on the inland road through Ipswich and Armidale to see Bryan Dowling and Ross Gibson. I left the Turbo in Canberra and Bryan took me to the Centenary Celebrations at Warragul in Victoria in his Maserati Merak. There we attended the Centenary Ball with me dressed in an ill fitting dinner suit Bryan had hired for me and with my feet delicately clad in my motorcycle boots.

On the way back to Canberra we managed to pull the sump plug out of the Maser' on a bump on the main highway. Clearance was not one of the Maserati's strengths. That resulted in it being left at Gundagai with no oil in it while we hitched a ride back to Canberra in a potato truck.

I rode back to it early enough in the morning that I was able to supervise winching it on to a transport truck. I left Gundagai to set forth across Australia, with my first leg being the ride down the Murray Valley in a howling northerly and 38 degree heat. The difficult and drying conditions were alleviated by a skinny dip in a lonely part of the Murray River and lying around wet, in my underpants, reading Joseph Heller's book, "Good as Gold" for a while. It is not a patch on his classic "Catch 22".

The ride across our great country was punctuated with a stay in Adelaide, where I went to the races with Adelaide's best known undertaker, Darrell Blackwell, and visited my old mentor, the party animal Charlie Roberts, and his wife Barbara.

Charlie and Barbara deserve some space in this chronicle, not because they had much to do with motorcycling but because they were important to my family and me. When Lynne and I and our burgeoning brood lived in Mount Lawley Charlie, Barbara and their two children, Chris' and Linda, moved into the house opposite. With his energy and his personality Charlie lit Woodsome Street up. His mother had been the "Queen of the Soldiers" during the First World War and the family were well to do when Charlie and his brother John were young. After their parents died Charlie and John managed to spend the family fortune on high living and travel so that Charlie had then to earn a living.

I do not know much about his early career. I know he married and fathered two boys, John and Tony. John went on to become the billionaire founder and chief of the international construction company, Multiplex. Barbara, Charlie's second wife, was part of a pioneering family from the south west.

Charlie never lost the ability to enjoy life. He was selling second hand cars from a yard in Albany Highway at the time he moved in and he was successful. He was generous and he believed in spreading his good fortune to others. He had the first television set in the street and his neighbours were always welcome to drop in to gawk at "Have Gun – Will Travel" and share a beer. Charlie was a wonderful host and Barbara stoically backed him up by making food for those he invited home and cleaning up the remains later.

When I held a "head wetting" to celebrate the arrival of one of our children Charlie would turn up with tray loads of expensive food. He was always the life of the party. When Charlie's fortunes took a turn for the worse and he left for greener fields in South Australia we stayed in touch. I could not pass through Adelaide without seeing Charlie and Barb'.

When I arrived in Adelaide the Turbo needed a service. Mr. Honda was very nice about it but he explained that they could not possibly fit in such a service until next Tuesday, by which time I was due back in Perth. Charlie talked to the agent and they fitted it in next day. He was a persuasive man. I miss him but I still have the friendship of his son Chris' and Chris's wife Judy. Chris' also went on to great things as CO of the SAS regiment and, later, CO of Northern Command.

On that trip I rode from Nullarbor Homestead to Perth in one day. It is about 1650km. I set off before first light and rode to the cliffs of the Great Australian Bight on the way to the Western Australian border. In those days I was addicted to nicotine so I stopped for an early morning fag at one of the parking bays. In the pale pink early morning light I looked out from the cliff's edge at the Southern Ocean, which was a deep magenta in colour. It was an enchanting scene made more enchanting when I found that, at the bottom of the vertical cliff on the edge of which I was perched, directly under my eyrie, there were dozens of dolphins surfing the big Southern Ocean waves to the cliff's face. It was a sight that, to coin a cliché, I will never forget. The wine dark sea, the pale, pastel sky and the sporting animals surfing in to the base of the cliff and then turning to ride the rip tides on both sides of their surfing lane out for hundreds of metres to do it all again in a continuous double swirl was, a piece of nature's wonder and majesty.

I breakfasted at Eucla and headed for Norseman. Then I turned north for Coolgardie.

When I arrived there to refuel it was late afternoon and I was heading east into a setting sun. I could not see much so I stopped and bought an ice cream and waited for the sun to go down.

When it finally dipped below the horizon I got back onto the trusty Turbo for the last leg. On the plain I had darted along at about 150 -160kph and I recognised that I would not be able to keep that pace up in more civilised parts after it became dark.

Then difficulties arrived. Up until then I had only ridden during daylight hours so I was not aware that my headlight was so badly adjusted that even on low beam it was directly into the eyes of oncoming traffic. Traffic coming towards me flashed their lights at me and even turned spotlights onto me making seeing where I was going impossible. I had two alternatives. Either stop and wait until the next day or turn off my headlights when a vehicle approached and ride to dodge to the left of the oncoming vehicle.

I stopped and tried to adjust the beams but it was not possible. The light was built into the fairing and it was not made to be adjusted by an amateur. Now under ordinary circumstances I would have sought a bed for the night or camped but the circumstances were not normal. I was courting Kaye and I wanted to see her so I continued. Each time a car or truck approached I turned off my lights and headed to the left of the oncoming pair of dimmed lights. It was all a bit difficult, probably dangerous and distinctly scary and as it proved it was all a waste.

I finally rode into South Perth to the apartment I was sharing with Nick and my daughter Jacqueline at about 11pm. It goes without saying that they were not home and I had no key. Despite my several day's facial growth and a frame that had exerted itself for many hours in riding gear and would certainly be smelly I set forth for Kaye's place in Subiaco using my parking lights. I was buoyed by the thought that she would be pleased to see me even if I was not my normal, cleanly shaven, after shave lotioned and debonair self.

I was wrong. She was not home either. I sat in her courtyard smoking cigarettes until nearly 2am before I gave up. Then I went home to find my juniors were still not there. I was exhausted. I pulled the air mattress out of the pool and collapsed on it in my riding gear and slept the sleep of the buggered. My children turned up next morning. They were not even slightly contrite, "Dad, you should have let us know you were on your way". Kaye said something similar.

Chapter 14.
Nick's First Trip.

By 1985 Nick had upgraded to a 4 cylinder 550cc Suzuki so we rode north together to Karratha to visit my second daughter, and Nick's sister, Rebecca, her partner Wayne and their two young children. After a shaky start Nick also became hooked on two-wheeled travel over long distances. He is still a devotee as you will read. On our first night we shared a meal in Carnarvon where, as it turned out, Nick was a friend of the lady proprietor. We cooled off in Peter's Creek after a hot spell of riding and we found that we were compatible travelling companions – largely due to Nick taking most things in his stride. The trip was a success and cemented a motorcycling and travelling friendship that endures.

Chapter 15.
Around the North by BMW.

In 1986 my darling second wife, Kaye, then did me one of the great favours of my life by producing a son – Hans. I love all seven of my children and I do not wish to single Hans out for any special recognition, or to suggest that he has attributes that are somehow superior to Lynne's six marvellous offspring. However, becoming a father for the seventh time at the age of 53, when I was already a grandfather, was certainly special.

At about that time I was travelling to Canberra quite frequently, by air, to work on a new hotel and on a medium rise apartment block in Kingston for Ross Gibson and his syndicate. Bryan Dowling was the architect for both.

Late one Friday afternoon, just before I was due to fly back to Perth a friend, and one of Ross's syndicate, Tony, rang me at Bryan's office and said he was at the home of the Chilean Ambassador to Australia. He was there to buy the ambassador's Mercedes, because the ambassador was leaving Australia, when he noticed a large motorcycle in the garage and wondered if I would like to buy it. He did not know what it was or anything much about it except that it looked pretty good to him and it was likely to be a "good buy". I told him that I was out of time and that I had a plane to catch.

Within ten minutes he turned up and dragged me downstairs where I found the Ambassador of Chile to Australia and a near new K100RS BMW complete with panniers. I was under the hammer of time so in just a few minutes the ambassador and I agreed that Tony would broker a fair price for the bike and I would buy it.

I told Nick about it and he decided he would like to have the bike. Then, on my next Canberra trip, I found another, almost identical, BMW in a second-hand yard at Fyshwick that was only just run in and bought that also. It had been purchased in Germany by a Canberra dentist and ridden around for only a couple of weeks. It was also set up for touring. Nick and I were on our way to our first Australian odyssey.

We both flew to Adelaide with Peter Canaway. Peter, then an associate of the Bruechle Gilchrist and Evans group, had to check some precast concrete in Adelaide so I went with him. He was working on our projects in Canberra at the time. He later became Managing Director of the group I founded and, with his organisational skills, he and his team made it bigger and more financially successful.

In Adelaide we picked up a hire car and drove to Canberra via the Murray Valley and the Kosciusko national park. We even climbed Mount Kosciusko, Australia's tallest peak. It is not an inspiring climb.

In Canberra we stayed with my old mate John Devitt, a man that we would all like to think was the mould for all Australians (I would that it was so) and took delivery of the bikes.

After a couple of days taking in the sights of Canberra and sampling a range of beers Nick and I took off for Queensland, rode up to the Daintree River, crossed it on the barge that transports vehicles over it and rode onto Cape York Peninsula on a slippery and rough road – a road that was difficult on two heavily laden road bikes. I knew I was going to fall off – I just did not know when. I was wrong again – thankfully. It is a wonderful part of the world and I could go on and on about it.

After the Daintree rain forest and the Mossman Gorge, in the cold river of which Nick had to stay for much longer than he intended, because a tourist crowd turned up just as he had decided he had had enough of swimming with nothing on while I stood on the bank in my jeans and chortled - we rode across to the main Adelaide to Darwin road, the Stuart Highway, through Mount Isa and Julia Creek.

Although this is not the story of that trip I want to tell you about a rare spectacle we saw on the plains east of Julia Creek. The plains were long, bare and flat with a single, pole mounted telephone line and a wire fence alongside the straight road. The road, the fence and the telephone line faded to pin points on the horizon under the influence of the wonderful invention of perspective. When we rode across these plains they were host to clouds of white moths or butterflies. There were at least ten per cubic metre for many kilometres. What they were doing there, why they were there and what they planned on their progeny eating on that barren plain I have no idea, but there they were, clouds of them hitting our helmets with soft sputters and clogging up the helmet vents. It was like riding in warm snowflakes. We had ridden in an environment that might be unique.

When we hit the Stuart Highway we turned north for Darwin where the bikes had to be serviced. On the way to Darwin we stopped at a place that Tony Brand and I had found to be an enchantment when we drove from Darwin to Perth via "The Rock" of Uluru, the Olgas and the far flung centres of Docker River, Giles, Cosmo Newberry and Laverton about 35 years ago.

That place was, and is, Mataranka, on the Roper River. When Tony and I were there it was an outpost with its hot spring of pellucid water and its river containing salt water crocodiles and barramundi. At that time there were a few people living in tents, including a girls school from Melbourne out learning about the hardships of the outback, and a tiny, outdoor bar where we hardy travellers slaked our well earned thirsts after trolling for barra' in our little inflatable. I rowed – Tony fished. We fitted in nicely sleeping in the back of the Range Rover on an air mattress as we were.

When Nick and I pulled in it was, alas, no longer an outback post but was civilised. It had been used as the setting for a film (We of the Never Never) and it was now popular. There were caravans galore, motel units, a restaurant and all the conveniences (?) of the modern world. It goes without saying that although the spring and the river were still there it was, for me, not as good. It lacked the ambience of yore and it was overrun with people. We settled into a motel room, dunked our weary bodies in the hot spring pool and then trundled down for a beer in the beer garden where we talked to a large and tough gentleman who told us that he had swapped his BMW for a Harley because the BMW was too quiet and too reliable. Nothing went wrong and nothing fell off. "It wasn't a motorbike".

In Darwin we were met by cyclone "Kaye" who made our stay there while the bikes were serviced bloody wet and uncomfortable and who then followed us all the way from Darwin down to Geraldton and rained on us every day. My intellect tells me that cyclones cannot have personalities and that they are random acts of nature but on the evidence available cyclone Kaye seems to me to have been personal and personally retributive. My wife Kaye was unhappy about me not being home for Hans's first birthday and considered it a sure sign of a lack of parental responsibility. What she did then I do not know. What I do know is that she appears to have managed to call up a cyclone in her name to teach me a lesson. Cyclone Kaye demonstrates one of her many abilities. It was a superbly vindictive act for such a small sin as missing a birthday.

On that trip we attempted to get out to the fabled attractions of Cape Keraudren but we failed. There were washaways that were impassable on our heavily laden BMWs and when we attempted to skirt them on loose sand tracks we became bogged and had to turn the great beasts around in the knee deep powder before we could return whence we had come.

It was disappointing and muscle wrenching. We did manage to get out to the Loop on the Murchison River on the BMWs for a visit to that spectacular valley, even though Cyclone Kaye rained on us most of the way. Our trip was great, there were many highlights and lowlights, and Nick and I confirmed our lasting relationship but, once again, it is another story.

Searching for but not finding a suitable route to Cape Keraudren in 1987.

Chapter 16.
Kaye on the Road.

Kaye was already a reasonably seasoned biker's bird by the time I rolled into Perth on the BMW. She had ridden with me from Perth to Kalgoorlie and back on the Turbo and we had gone down to Nornalup on it for a few days with friends one Easter. The ride back had been in diabolical conditions. The rain poured down, as it often seems to manage to do at Easter, and the main road was packed with slowly moving caravans. Passing was hazardous and accompanied by showers of ice cold water from the wheels of the passed vehicles.

We arrived home frozen and soaked. A hot spa bath improved things to such an extent that Kaye said she had quite enjoyed the trip, especially the afternoon run through the Karri forest to Nornalup on the way down, in balmy conditions. She was prepared to try again.

Heartened by her forbearance I suggested a ride north to warmer climes on the BMW and she agreed. We rode up to Exmouth in easy stages via Geraldton and Coral Bay stopping along the way to sample the local delights. However we came home in only one day with the final stretch covered in the dark in a rain storm. Hans was still a young baby and Kaye was desperate to get him back into her clutches.

You have to admire a woman who can not only conjure up a cyclone to demonstrate her displeasure but can also sit on the back of a motorcycle for 1300k, the distance from Exmouth to Perth, in one stretch. She also sat quietly on the back while I wrestled the BMW down the loose sand, wheel ruts with the occasional snake slithering along them that then constituted the road to Yardie Creek and the terrifying track with huge falls both sides that was then the Charles Knife Road. Today the Charles Knife is spectacular and rough. Then it was diabolical, loose and heart stopping. No murmur of complaint was made by my lady. She might have just been too petrified to say anything.

On the ride home it started to rain at Geraldton so I suggested dropping anchor at a motel for the night. Kaye would not hear of such wimpish behaviour. We had to press on to the precious infant. That was the signal for it to pour in earnest. As the rain increased and darkness fell I had trouble seeing the road in my headlight beam through my rain spattered and fogged up visor. I indulged in the old trick of following the tail lights of cars with windscreen wipers but the rain was so heavy that even the cars could not see properly. Several times the car I was following veered off the road with me following. The road edge cobbles usually gave me the hint that all was not well and I would slow to a crawl and pick my way back to the road where I continued to crawl until another car I could follow had passed us.

After our difficult and dangerous ride we arrived home quite late with boots full of water and wet underclothing to find the little man asleep and not even slightly interested in parents he had not seen for a couple of weeks. When all had settled down again Kaye explained to me with an assured clarity that having two motorcycles was having at least one too many so, with regret and a sense of loss, the BMW was sold. I had to hold onto the Turbo. It is nearly unique.

Chapter 17.
Hans on the Road.

When Hans, who is twenty one as I write this in 2007, was seven Kaye went away for a holiday. I loaded up the Turbo's saddle bags, stuck my beloved son on the rear of the dual seat and we went to Geraldton. We had a lovely time once I learnt that I had to tie him to me because he insisted on falling asleep. When Kaye returned she was a little unimpressed that I had risked her beloved infant on a motorcycle but as no damage had been suffered she soon stopped threatening to kill me if I was ever so stupid again.

Chapter 18.
Nick and I Plan a Trip.

For a period after selling the BMW I rode the old Honda Turbo and then Nick and I decided to ride across to Melbourne and around Tasmania. The Turbo was not as reliable as it had been. Because silly things such as fuses kept packing up at most inconvenient times and places I concluded it was not the machine for the trip. Nick's BMW was also ageing and giving trouble, so we both bought bikes for the trip. I bought a near new 750cc, V4, VFR Honda and Nick bought a 1000cc CBR, in line 4 Honda, the latest incarnation of my old Bol D'or. When we had put together all the tools and bits and pieces that we had to take we set off. Our first stop was Manjimup to visit my old uncle, Wally.

Chapter 19.
Wally.

Walter Bruechle junior, who has died since this last visit to him, was a character. He was brought up in the Kalgoorlie goldfields with my father early in the twentieth century at a time when life was tough. He always looked up to my Dad, his older brother.

Wally was a courageous, tough and independent man with the fatal flaw of bad timing and a very stubborn streak. He was not prone to giving up. He worked in the Manjimup area as a young man and later in the goldfields during the depression. There he married and had children. The children did not unite Wally and his wife Mavis, which was a pity.

When the Second World War broke out he volunteered to join the army although he was past the age when men were usually accepted. He was still in Australia when the war ended but, with his innate sense of adventure, he volunteered to serve with the British Commonwealth Occupation Forces in Japan. There he managed to make friends with many Japanese, whom he liked and with whom he empathised, and to get into several scrapes.

We always looked forward to Wally's parcels to the family because they contained treasures such as silks and chocolate. When he returned he decided he wanted to go onto the land, which the government of the time was encouraging returned servicemen to do. After going through apprenticeships at dairy farms at Cookernup, and later in Roleystone, he was duly rewarded with his own dairy farm near Manjimup by a grateful government. Wally had returned to his spiritual home.

The dairy farm was seven miles out of Manjimup on the Seven Day Road, not far from the famous Fonty's Pool. Once he was established Wally found he had the ability to grow a luxurious clover crop, or to produce brilliantly colourful and tasty Delicious apples, or to have his herd produce high quality butter fat one year after that particular item's peak had passed or one year before it arrived and he nearly always delivered into an uninterested market or a glut.

It was not an easy life and Mavis finally quit, took the children and left him and the farm to it. Wally then embarked on a series of adventures of one sort and another. His story is one of gallantry overlain by undue optimism, boyish enthusiasm, bad luck and a refusal to let the facts interfere with his wishful thinking. He was, of course, a rabid left winger who believed in the inherent evil of the moneyed classes and the inherent virtue of the "working classes". He wrote left wing letters to local, State and National papers that they often published. He was very lovable – but difficult.

I have many memories of my Uncle Wally – the ever ebullient, ever optimistic and ever doomed to disappointment Wally. Early one morning when I was an eighteen year old student dressed in a snow white wind cheater (the student rig of the day), trousers that had been carefully ironed to a crease that could have cut butter and a highly polished pair of Julius Marlow moccasins, feeling as self important as only the young or those who have never grown up can, I alighted onto Perth railway station from the Armadale line in early morning, early summer sunshine. There I ran into Wally.

He was dressed in scruffy working clothes covered in dried mud. Over his shoulder he had the piece de resistance – a hessian bag that was dripping blood. Apparently late the previous afternoon a passing neighbour stopped and told him that he was going to Perth for a couple of days. That sounded like fun to Wally so he decided to come along. He milked the cows and joined Bert on his trip. Naturally he could not come empty handed so he had slaughtered and cleaned a calf. The bag contained its remains. He greeted me with "I knew that if I stood here long enough I would see someone I knew".

He wanted to know how to get to my father. Wally and I then tramped through the streets of Perth city dripping blood and followed by an enchanted cloud of flies as we wended our way to my father's work place in upper Hay Street. I was in an agony of embarrassment that I might be seen with him. Now, of course, I would be delighted to be part of such a spectacle. On that day Wally taught me not to be too concerned with the figure I cut and that true honesty and enthusiasm have much to recommend them. As I said earlier – he was a lovable man.

One April, after Dad had died, I took some leave from the Architectural Division and rode the Thunderbird down to Manji' to help Wally hull his clover crop. This consisted of towing a roller covered in sheep skins behind a tractor over drying clover. The spiked seed pods adhered to the sheep skins. They were scraped off and put through a machine that shook out the seeds. It "hulled" them. There was, naturally, a glut of clover seed that year.

Wally insisted on me taking him to a dance, miles away, over the rough and gravely roads of the time late one afternoon on the Thunderbird. He had a marvellous time dancing with old flames while I was fed the coldest of shoulders by the local young belles. I had a thoroughly miserable night. Then I had the pleasure of riding home over those terrible roads by the bouncing light of a none too powerful headlight. On the back Wally kept falling asleep. He was exhausted. Next day Wally waxed enthusiastic about the great night we both had. I did not disabuse him.

Wally decided he needed a shed and when he found out that there was a collection of sheds, of various types that had been built in the Pemberton railway yards, for sale by tender he decided to put up his hand. He carefully worked out what he thought each of the sheds were worth and he put in tenders on each of them for half what he believed they would fetch, hoping to win one. He was awarded the lot. I spent several days with him dismantling them, loading the spoils onto his old International truck and transporting them from Pemberton to his farm where they reposed in a mouldering heap for years. I drove the laden truck through the spectacular karri forest many times with Wally either waxing enthusiastic about the trees and the light, the bird life, literature, the civilisation that was Japan or anything else that came into his mind, or sleeping while I hung grimly over the steering wheel of the International and clashed gears in the non-synchromesh gear box. At the time

I thought it was all a dreadful trial for a young man but, you know, I can still see the light filtering through the trees on those drives and I can still hear Wally telling me things and sharing his experiences with me. The young have so little understanding.

One of the things that we did together was to visit Diamond Tree. I wanted to climb it on its ladder of rungs driven into the trunk. Wally thought that that was not only a waste of energy, it was also unnecessarily hazardous. I persuaded him to try. Once he started he realised that there was a different perspective, one he had never seen before, as he rose. When he arrived at the cabin at the top of the tree he looked out over his beloved Karri forest and a new world was opened to him, and to me. I did not realise what I had started at the time.

After the dairy farm became too much for him he got a job fire watching so he spent several of his later years sitting in cabins, by himself, which would have been difficult for such a gregarious man, on tops of karri trees making sure his beloved bush was safe.

At the time Nick and I invaded him he was well into his eighties and suffering from emphysema – a product of many years of smoking "roll your owns". He was still smiling, writing left wing letters to the newspapers and optimistic. He was delighted with Nick who, he said, looked very much like his beloved brother Hans.

Chapter 20.
Another Crash.

After spending a whole morning with Wally, which put us behind schedule, we proceeded down through the Karri forest and I fell off at fairly high speed. I do not want to dwell on my fall because I am not proud to have had it but Nick tells me I should provide some information about it.

My bike was heavily laden and, because we were late, I - and it was me leading - was travelling too fast for the conditions. Half way around a right hand sweeping bend in the Karri forest north of Northcliffe, when I was well into my "line", I encountered a very wide caravan heading in the opposite direction. I had to change direction and then settle back into a tighter line still. At that stage I saw what I thought was a patch of loose material on the new line so I stood the bike up to avoid sliding and then realized I could not take the bend.

As I took to the gravel on the edge of the road my last thought was "I'll just ride through this". It was unfounded optimism. I fell off at 140kmh. As it turned out that wrote the bike off. It also resulted in the socket attached to the shoulder blade that holds the top of my right upper arm bone being snapped off and a bit of skin being taken from my legs but I was relatively unscathed. I can still see the gravel racing past my face 50mm away at over 100kmh. Without a good helmet I would have ground a great deal of my face away and without a good jacket I would have lost more flesh.

When I came to a halt I realized I had a broken bone. It hurt a lot and I had trouble moving. About that time a very concerned Nick turned up at my side. I told him that I was OK but that something was broken. The world swirled around me for a time with concerned people worrying about me, especially Nick, but I was dazed and the pain was causing me to lose concentration. I felt removed from it all.

An ambulance took me to the Manjimup hospital after what seemed forever and there I stayed until Kaye came down next day to pick up the broken mess. She brought Nick with her. He had ridden his CBR back to Perth the previous afternoon and came down with Kaye to ride the V4 back. The insurance company had one look at it and decided it could not be repaired.

Although this is only background to the Kununurra trip I cannot resist a detour to tell you about one of the things that happened in Manjimup Hospital. After X rays and bandaging and when I was feeling less than terrific an aged and obviously bored patient named - wouldn't you know it – Paddy, wandered in and asked why I was there. I told him I had fallen off a motorcycle and he asked where I had been heading. When I told him Melbourne he pointed out, probably with reasonable justification, that I was going in the wrong direction. I told him that I had come through Manji' to see Wally Bruechle. He fixed me with his eagle eye and said "You know, there are only two real bastards in Manjimup and Wally Bruechle is BOTH of them". It's nice to be part of a family with a high profile.

The VFR looking more than slightly worse for wear.

Chapter 21.
Nothing Daunted.

After recovering, because my stubborn streak is wider than my self protection intelligence is deep, I bought another near new VFR, V4 Honda, this time in Karratha, and Nick, Hans and I drove up to pick it up stopping along the way to sample the delights of swimming in gorges and camping under the stars.

We had never given up on the Tasmanian trip and after a couple of years we decided it was time. As Nick's CBR was starting to age I sold him the V4 I had bought to replace the machine I had written off and purchased a new, injected 800cc V4. On those bikes we rode across Australia again, put the bikes on the "Devil Cat", got off at Launceston and rode away into the sunset.

If you want to know about that trip read the book that Nick wrote about it. To whet your appetite I will tell you that the two days we took to ride from Adelaide to Melbourne were the wettest days for 100 years in that area and I had to ride without rear vision mirrors.

Still not satisfied, although age and falls had taken their toll and I was not as limber, as quick nor as brave as I used to be, and I ache a fair bit, I rode to Exmouth with Nick and a Singapore Airlines pilot named Mike Bernoulli. We all fell off in unison and in slow motion on a particularly nasty piece of the road riding out to the Loop on the Murchison River. Very disappointing. Nick and I had ridden to the Loop before, on the BMW's, without such an ignominious result.

Stopping in Cocklebiddy on the Nullarbor, en route to Melbourne and Devonport.

Falling off in sync – the road to the Loop in Kalbarri where we all went down.

Chapter 22.
Dubai.

In August 1997 I turned 65 and left the consulting practice I had inaugurated in 1961. Shortly before I retired, in June 1997 and while I was still the managing director of Bruechle, Gilchrist and Evans, Derek Robson, then managing director of Multiplex, asked me to go with him to Dubai to see if we could arrive at economical structural solutions for a pair of towers that were proposed for Sheikh Mohammed al Maktoum, a leader in Dubai and in the Gulf States, in an endeavour to win the contract to build one, or both, of them.

The chances were not good. There were already several major European and Gulf contractors who were well established and had local track records, and the structures for the towers had already been designed and documented by the international consulting group Hyder.

Suggesting changes to those structures, already designed and documented, was not going to be greeted with anything but negativity. I started coming up with approaches that would be easier and quicker to build and Derek did all the difficult things – arranging financial backing, finding the necessary local partner, tapping sub-contractors and suppliers and convincing them that we were substantial, putting in bids for cranes, getting together a team of experienced local building experts who were prepared to enter into contracts should we be successful, finding out where site facilities could be obtained and generally putting the necessary team together.

Derek performed brilliantly and convinced the project managers, Turner Steiner of the USA that we were not only able to build better and faster than the establishment but we could also build cheaper.

To cut a long story short Multiplex, which became NASA Multiplex, were awarded the contract to build what was then the tallest tower in Europe and the Middle East, using a revised structure with much of it prefabricated off site using principles developed on office towers successfully built in Perth. I was asked to go to the Gulf and act as design manager to get the re-designs through the design team, Turner Steiner and the local authorities. After much heartburn and snide manoeuvring and with detailed design back-up from my old firm the changes to the structure were successfully made and we built the tower more rapidly than anything had been built in Dubai before.

What, I hear you ask, has this to do with motorcycling? Patience!

The main supervisor of the structure for Turner Steiner was Martin Adams, an English engineer and an avid motorcyclist who happily rode through the mad scramble that was then Dubai traffic, with its no speed limits and its dodgem car melee, on his big trail bike BMW.

He was happy enough to lend the bike to me so I had some exciting rides on it with its light front wheel that kept lifting off the deck. Then, when the project got under way, one of NASA MX's leading foremen, David Miller, turned out to have a triple Triumph and he, also, was prepared to let me borrow it. Martin on his BMW and I on my borrowed triple Triumph rode across the desert on a good road to Fujairah and stayed the night in what turned out to be a dry hotel. Next day we rode back to Dubai but in desert wind conditions. The wind gusted viciously causing the bikes to veer suddenly. However that was not the main difficulty. The wind also swept up the desert sands so that the road could not be seen. We flew blind for quite long periods. Exciting and tiring stuff. Even in the Gulf I had opportunities to ride.

Later Martin, on a new BMW, T-boned a car that turned in front of him on a main road and he and his secretary flew over the bonnet of the car and landed heavily, breaking many bones. Both survived. Dubai traffic is not for the faint hearted.

Chapter 23.
Choosing Kununurra.

Although what I have written leaves much unsaid and my selection of anecdotes has been arbitrary that brings us more or less up to date and to the decision for the old man to have what is probably his last long ride. We thought about Darwin but we settled on Kununurra because Nick could only take three weeks off from his advertising business and we did not want Hans, who wanted to come also, to miss too much of his university course. We could get to Kununurra in a week even though we planned to stop and explore along the way. Then Nick's wife Rachel and Kaye could fly up to join us for a week at Lake Argyle. That left us with a week to get home by a different route.

I will not go into how we arrived at the format of Nick, my eldest son who was born in 1961, and Hans, my youngest son who was born in 1986, driving the Range Rover towing a trailer full of spare tyres, water, an ice box containing beer and fresh vegetables and a pile of camping gear and me riding the V4. It is enough to say that it was not Nick's idea but he was prepared to forego the ride to keep his young brother company and share the driving.

Arranging a trip takes time and planning. Distances had to be calculated that were possible for an aged biker. Maps were pored over and information gained on places of interest that we had not visited before. Finally an itinerary was agreed that we thought we could meet without undue risk to life or limb.

Accommodation was booked in far flung places, aeroplane tickets for Kaye and Rachel were ordered, camping and towing equipment we had was checked and replaced where necessary, the trailer we had previously towed across the north of Australia to Queensland and then back to Uluru and across the Nullarbor was refurbished for the trip (not as well as it should have been as it turned out) and the ageing Range Rover was given a complete set of new hoses and otherwise readied for the trip. It took quite a bit of time and several dollars. Fully equipped (?) we set out on the morning of Saturday 16 July 2005.

Chapter 24.
Day 1. Saturday 16 July 2005.
Perth to Meekatharra.

I was a bit nervous about such a long first day before I had time to settle into the rhythm of travel on the bike but it was necessary to cover nearly 800km on that day if we were to meet our schedule. We left at 7.45am after a final pack up and headed off with the thermometer registering an unfriendly 11 degrees C under an overcast sky.

The first part of the trip was uneventful as we wended our way through the Swan Valley past the vineyards and the many restaurants that have blossomed in it. The temperature started to rise, the sun shone through the clouds in patches, my hands stopped getting colder and life improved.

I sped up and left the boys behind as the smoothly running bike and I climbed up into the hills. The temperature dropped a degree at a time until it was down to 8 and a heavy mist clouded everything. It was attractive but uncomfortable.

Then it started to rain and I found myself trapped behind one road train after another with each of them spraying up sheets of water, which limited my vision and made it next to impossible to pass without risking a head on collision. I became wet and very cold despite the good riding gear in which I was encased. After mature consideration on the matter I reached the, as I saw it then, entirely reasonable conclusion that the whole idea of riding to Kununurra was a confidence trick foisted on me by my unthinking sons who were then sitting in dry luxury, with the heater at full blast. I pulled into New Norcia and stiffly dismounted.

A short while later, after I had walked up and down and had thawed somewhat, the Range Rover turned up and we had breakfast. We then carried on to Dalwallinu, where we filled up again, in improving and slightly warmer weather and then on to Mount Magnet where we filled up again. So far so good. My temper, always a fragile beast, improved. I recovered from concentrating purely on how cold, wet and miserable I was and, inside my helmet, I started to ponder some of the mysteries of our world.

Why, I asked myself, does mankind (or to be more politically correct, personkind, or perhaps, humankind) appear to have such an innate instinct to form itself into tribal groups of one sort or another. The deep seated urge probably stems from the times in pre-history when the weak and slow naked apes needed to club together to murder the animals they wanted to eat, and to protect themselves from the stronger predators that wanted to murder them. That is understandable.

But why did the tribes then fight with each other as they did and still do? Where did this destructive streak come from and what use does it now serve? With the discovery of the cultivation of food, and from that marvellous discovery the opportunity for people to live as groups in the settled conditions which produced civilisations, why did the tribal urge to dominate not fade?

Because there are so many advantages in all humankind acting together as a team why have we fractured and why do the various groups fight with each other? Now we have all sorts of groupings, primarily based on ethnicity and religion. Most of them are far from benign and many of them are completely pernicious.

Humankind's history is littered with different groups attacking each other. What primal instinct drove Alexander the Great to overrun the known world, slaughtering as he went? What possible long term advantage could he or his followers have gained? Why did Genghis Khan do something similar? Why do we remember acts of war and brutality as heroic episodes and often revel in them when we should, really, offer apologies that we are part of a species that indulges in such dreadful activities? What destructive tribal quirk drove

Adolph Hitler to believe that the Romanys and the Slavic and Jewish races were inferior and needed to be exterminated so that the Germanic tribes, who were worthy inheritors of the earth, could prosper? Why did the long suffering peoples of Russia and its satellites allow Stalin to treat them so badly with his NKVD, his GULags and his belief that he was entitled to be in absolute control? Why did, and do, hoards of people follow these, and similar, destructive megalomaniacs?

The urge to destruction is still rampant on our one and only globe from major, so called "ethnic cleansings", to punch ups between the fans of different football clubs. It is surely one of humankind's worst traits. Once it might have been useful to keep numbers down to sustainable levels so that we did not poison the world or eat ourselves into starvation as various civilisations have but as we have already succeeded in now being well on the way to poisoning our globe anyway and as there is really no shortage of food, only a rotten distribution system, what purpose does it now serve and, more importantly, can we eradicate it from our natures and stop its destructive and unbelievably wasteful effects?

 Are the differences between various groups that now exist due to their different religions or have the religions sprung from a desire to delineate differences between the tribes?

Why do religions survive despite efforts to wipe them out? The communist experiments of the USSR and China failed to kill off the religions and they have recovered ground, although some – consider the Christian religion – are fading in the western democratic worlds.

Why do groups who live in comfortable circumstances retain hatreds that are hundreds of years old as they do? Hatreds that are often carried to new countries. Why? What makes the Chechens consider that it is reasonable to kill school children in Moscow or a few fanatical Arabs consider that wrecking two of mankind's great high rise building achievements and killing thousands, as they did when they destroyed Yamasaki's World Trade Centre, is a worthy objective?

I was lucky enough to have met and held discussions with the great Minuro Yamasaki on two occasions. He told me that when he was asked what Yamasaki meant at a seminar he said it meant "Beyond the mountain" but a friend of his told the audience a closer literal translation was "Over the hill".

He was a modest genius with a quiet and self deprecating sense of humour and he was a creator. I am glad he had died before the horrible act that killed his buildings was perpetrated. He, as a creator, would have understood the drives to destroy that are so apparent in so many humans even less than I do.

As I rode along I came to the conclusion that there are many specimens of the naked ape who are destructive animals by nature and enjoy destruction for its own sake. Many naked apes look for excuses to destroy because it is part of their nature. It was a frightening, saddening thought. I hope it is wrong but the evidence says it is not. The majority must not follow leaders who want to dominate and are prepared to destroy to achieve domination.

Without followers megalomaniacs cannot thrive. However – if a destructive leader does, or leaders do, achieve a following and decide to dominate for racial or religious reasons have we devout cowards any alternative but to fight back? Is there a group, or are there groups that are set on domination now? If there are should the rest of us attempt to appease them or should we let them know that we will resist with force if necessary? It is a pity Neville Chamberlain is not around to ask. Am I being unduly pessimistic and if we act in a conciliatory way will those set on domination see the light and abandon their destructive approaches? The record says they will not.

At Cue we paused to do a lap of the town. We found, to my delight, that the old Men's Club that had been a tumble down wreck when Cyril, Ken and I first visited the town in 1967, and that had had such famous frequenters, in its hey day, as Herbert Hoover when he was still an important, youthful mining engineer, was returned to its former glory and was now the Cue Shire Offices. Hoover's career path took an unfortunate, downward turn after he gave up mining. He was elected to be the President of the US of A.

We also found, to my horror, that the two storey, corrugated iron manse, which is a gothic masterpiece and that was in good order and being used when Paul Bennett and I went through the town in the 70s was derelict and badly in need of love. This unique building deserves better.

When Cue was a centre of mining activity the State saw fit to build some fine buildings there and they still exist in good order. They are worth visiting. The Government Architects near the end of the nineteenth century, George Temple Poole and Richard Jewell, left many worthwhile buildings throughout the State. When the problems of travel over 100 years ago and the difficulties of taking material and labour supplies to remote sites are considered their creations are all the more meritorious. There was obviously heart and optimism in the population of that time.

The boys and I mulled over the idea of going out to Big Bell where Paul and I had camped all those years ago to look, once again, at the great pit but it is now a working mine, so much has changed. We would probably not have been welcome and we were running short of time. After a final lap of the town on the motorcycle I headed for Meekatharra under ominous grey clouds that were, however, tinged with hopeful white. These hung over me for long periods and the temperature dropped again. I arrived in Meeka' in the late afternoon, closely followed by the boys.

I was in pretty good shape for an ancient who had just ridden nearly 800km. We finished the afternoon off enjoying several cans of beer under a spectacular sunset and a dust free sky that glowed. A few beers do not bring out the best in the Bruechle boys so that by the time we cleaned up for dinner the, mostly insulting, puns were flying.

Out-back township dinners used to consist of a large, overcooked steak, covered in onions with a wilting salad on the side of the plate. Things are different now. We had a chilli prawn starter and washed our excellent meals down with a Margaret River red. Once it would then have been a visit to the bar or straight into bed. Now we sat around drinking more beer in a cloud of happy, alcohol fuelled camaraderie and watched the Eagles demolish the Lions on TV followed by "The Bill".

Chapter 25.
Day 2. Sunday 17 July 2005.
Meekatharra to Munjina.

After re-packing, settling bills and buying the mandatory stubby holder for Mr. Hans Bruechle – otherwise "the lump" (do not ask, it is a long story) – we left the motel at 8am. The temperature was 10 degrees C and there was not a cloud in the pale blue and light gold sky. There was no service station on the way out of town, as I assumed there would be, so I had to U turn across the main street to return to the one I knew was on the road in. This attracted the attention of a large, brown dog that either liked motorcycles and wanted to get closer to one or did not like motorcycles and wanted one as a trophy. He attacked the front wheel and took absolutely no notice of me explaining to him that either he was to go away or I would be forced to run over him, even though I said it in quite a loud, clear voice.

He was as unimpressed as I was with the sound of laughter from the Range Rover following me. I reflected on the value of family solidarity and what a comfort it is when one has a problem. Parents are lucky when they have devoted children who help out with good humour when they, the parents, are being harassed.

Once the tanks were refilled we left with me riding into a fairly low sun. Glass and quartz glinted each side of the road. Diamonds shone in the distance on the road surface itself and then changed from bright, white lights in a static surface to blurs 5m from my front wheel. It was cool but the sun warmed me.

I stopped at Kumarina for fuel and the boys turned up a short time later. We breakfasted, drank coffee and then took off for Mount Newman, where we found a service station and filled up again.

It had been a fair while since I had spent any time in Mount Newman and we decided that we would not ruin that record. When Mount Newman was little more than a name my team designed housing in precast concrete for Leightons, one of Australia's biggest contractors, who used the designs for a design and construct contract, which they won. Several hundred houses were built quickly and economically. Now the town is diverse and quite a metropolis, but it is not the pioneering town I first knew. Although it is undoubtedly a very nice town we did not come north for towns and we decided that there were better environments for us to enjoy in the limited time we had available.

The road from Newman to Munjina, where we had booked a motel room, is spectacular. Red hills surmounted by crowns of red stone laid in layers with random vertical joints are on both sides of an excellent road that winds between them, providing motorcyclists with a route of interest and riding excitement. Some hills are bare. Others have yellow/grey-green balls of Spinifex dotting them. Under a clear cool sky it was an enjoyable ride.

In the middle of the afternoon we arrived at Munjina with my backside telling me that I had been sitting on a motorcycle for two days and that was long enough for now.

We settled in, had a couple of palate cleansing ales and set off to explore the area in the Range Rover.

Munjina gorge is not the world's very best gorge but it is beautiful with its red sand, its Spinifex and its white, twisted, sculptural trees.

As we were happily walking around and taking photographs we came across a caravan belonging to Beryl and Lou on a knoll, one of the hundreds of such conveyances that tour the north during winter. Great camping spot - if windy.

After a healthy and invigorating couple of hours we returned to the motel to wash some clothing, to indulge in a G&T at sundown, to eat and to play noisy and competitive cards.

Chapter 26.
Day 3. Monday 18 July 2005.
Karajini Park.

Today was spent in the superb Karajini Park, one of my favourite parts of the world and a place to which I have been re-drawn many times since I first saw it with Ken and Cyril. I have been there with all sorts of people, including Kaye, whom I made climb down into narrow and beautiful Hancock Gorge and swim in its ice cold pools. I have never had anyone fail to be impressed. It is grandly magnificent, colourful, peaceful and with surprises. I even had a dream at one time that I would build an office on a high tor between gorges and deal with the world by electronic links. These high tors are plateaux scattered with shiny, near black, rounded stones set on a base of solid, red, fine grained earth and with beautifully sculptural, twisted white stemmed eucalypts dotted about.

I was convinced, when I first climbed up to the top of one of the tors, that if Frank Lloyd Wright had visited such a tor Taliesin West would never have been put where it was in Arizona but would have been built in Karajini.

In the past it has been possible to drive through Yampire Gorge to the gorges in the western section of the park. Nick's map showed a track so we decided to go that way as I had several times in the past. We asked the attendant at Munjina if he knew of any problems with the road and he told us that he had not heard of any.

I should have known better of course. I learnt a long time ago that if you want to find the provenance of a monument in Rome, or why a strange building in Los Angeles has been built, you do not ask anyone standing under it unless that person is a tourist or a guide. Locals never know.

So we proceeded to the Yampire Gorge turn off. We were not daunted by a "No Entry" sign that had been flattened at the turn off as tyre tracks clearly indicated that many others had obviously not been daunted before us and into the gorge we went. There were washaways and flowing water. The driving was difficult as we navigated these, but all this did was to impel us intrepid adventurers, as we saw ourselves, and our trusty Range Rover on. We had reached the, not unreasonable, conclusion that as we got further into, and higher up, the gorge the stream flow would abate and the travelling would be easier. This conclusion turned out to be exactly wrong.

After stopping to rest the RR and to climb on our own feet to higher levels to take photographs and to look at the old asbestos workings we drove on into deeper and deeper streams and found a track that obviously had not been used for some time. It was not as I remembered it. Finally at one crossing water started coming in under the doors and we called it a day. At that spot there was a tree with "Yee Hah" carved into it and I think I have worked out why. Although the youngest and most adventurous soul of we three was all in favour of carrying on Nick and I had no ambition to be stuck 40km from nowhere. Then we had to turn the bloody vehicle around, on a narrow, water filled track with football sized boulders as the base, which had its moments. It was either that or drive in reverse back to the main road.

We drove out deflated by not having been able to drive through, but buoyed by the scenery and the isolation of the gorge. If you get to Karajini do not miss Yampire Gorge and climb its walls to higher levels for fabulous scenery. The next gorge we drove to, after driving through the old town of Wittenoom, was Wittenoom Gorge. The township was closed down by the government many years ago because, with its asbestos tailings and asbestos sheeting, it is a health hazard. So far, it has refused to die. The hardy souls who live there like it and, placed as it is on the wide, brown, flat plane at the base of the Hamersley Ranges, that is not hard to understand.

The layered rocks of Yampire Gorge. Imagine how long it has taken the creek to carve this gorge out, if you can. We humans are paltry, recent additions to the globe.

The Hamersley ranges are quite special. Not only do they have presence from a distance – they also have within them some of the world's most attractive gorges.

Wittenoom Gorge was the site of major blue asbestos mining and there was a town in the gorge, the foundations of which are still there. The town site can still be visited and many tourists camp there in amongst the stately white gums surrounded by rounded, red hills sparsely coated with small Spinifex mounds and by great mounds of mining rubble that the authorities, no doubt concerned about an outbreak of mesothelioma and a rash of victims suing them, have used to block all the roads up into the old mining areas. This is probably wise but the closures irritated an old biker who wanted another look at scenes he had visited years ago. The frustration of not being able to penetrate further into the old gorges was alleviated by a picnic lunch. The town in Wittenoom Gorge might be shut down but there is still a good deal of life amongst the tailings dumps.

Because the old tracks were blocked by mullock heaps there was nothing for it but to drive around the park and enter from the other side. This meant driving north along the folded Hamersley Ranges, which are spectacular, clad as they are in their misty grey greens and their dark reds, and well worth the drive along the flat, rutted and corrugated gravel road. Then we turned and

A closer look at the timeworn landscape of this ancient landscape.

entered from the west. It was a good drive with the only problem being that because of the time it absorbed there was not enough left to visit all that I would like to have seen again.

We managed to visit the dark, damp and mysterious Circular Pool and we walked part of the flat, layered stone and bush trails of Dales Gorge. We photographed the dashing, splashing nature's fountain that is Fortescue Falls with its backdrop of vertical, red stone cliffs glowing in the afternoon sunshine under a golden, incredibly clear sky.

Dales Gorge featuring Fortescue Falls in the late afternoon under a pale golden sky.

The boys had a swim in the bracingly cold pool above the Falls where Peter Knight and I showered under a small waterfall years ago while Paul Bennett took salacious movies on his Super 8, no doubt for sale in some market that it is better we ordinary people know nothing about. I told Paul that they would not be printed by Mr. Kodak who tended to be pretty straight laced about developing photographs of body appendages at the time. I was, as I so often am, wrong. Paul still has his movies.

The pool above Fortescue Falls in which Nick and Hans swam. It has been the scene of memorable swims on previous trips. It is beautiful.

Time and light started to run out. The park was as magnificent as I remembered it. The light was as clear and the colours as brilliant. The brightly orange – red stones forming the cliff faces are still layered in beautifully precise formations. The trees are still glowingly white stemmed and leaved in darkest green. Their branches and trunks are still twisted by the life force that drives them into sculptured shapes. The water that flows over Fortescue Falls and pools in ponds that are ringed in bright green ferns is still limpidly clear and the sky is still a golden shade of palest blue.

We drove back to Munjina as it grew dark. The boys were on a high from the day and their ice cold swim and vied with each other to take the best digital pictures of Venus rising in a sparklingly clear and darkening sky. It was a great and memorable day which we finished by eating several cans of mixed delights heated in our camp wok for dinner. We hit the sack early. Tomorrow we had quite a distance to cover.

The distances out here can be daunting.

The 'Yee Ha' tree.

Karijini presents so many different faces.

Having a well-earned drink after a long day on the road – Munjina.

Chapter 27.
Day 4. Tuesday July 19.
Munjina to Broome.

Today was going to be a testing day. The distance from Munjina to Broome, with byways, is nearly 900k. When we left it was 10C, and that soon fell to 9C. I suppose I should let you in on the secret as to how I knew the temperature then and at the other times I have given it in these chronicles. My V4 Honda has a thermometer that will tell me either the ambient temperature or the engine temperature at the push of a button on the dashboard. It is extremely handy, I could even say valuable in the extreme, to have a device that, when you are freezing your butt off, and you cannot feel or properly move your fingers anymore, lets you know exactly how cold it is and how hot the motor is.

Even though it was cool the run, under a clear pale sky with a few fluffy clouds adding interest, was great. The first section of road runs down the edge of the Hamersleys and then you turn and ride into banks of other hills. Some are starkly bare and some are softened by the unique, misty grey-green balls of Spinifex with their crowning haze of pale gold fronds.

Big brown eagles with their oversize, pyjama panted, feathered legs huddled over road kill and flapped off reluctantly as I approached. In warming weather the run was full of interest and the journey to South Hedland went by

Grey-green Spinifex with its halo of golden fronds is a unique Australian grass.

quickly. As we breakfasted at South Hedland we discussed whether or not we should spend any time at Port Hedland and decided against it. Broome was still a long way off. The next stop was Sandfire.

As I rode towards it on the good, paved road that it now is I reminisced about the night Paul Bennett and I had covered the same route but in torrential rain on a mud road in a previous incarnation of today's Range Rover.

We detoured out to Cape Keraudren because I wanted to show Paul its wonders even though it was dark and raining. We parked the Range and scrambled over the sharp, worn rocks covered in oysters, down onto the rippled flats that appear when the tide is out as it was then. We wandered around upsetting octopi with our torch light and watching silver fish skim across the surface of the low water in the channels as they attempted to escape predators.

When we finally turned for home we could not find the Range Rover. Our torch was giving out when we finally saw its reflection in the Range's windshield. I was beginning to think we would have to spend a wet night huddled up in a hole in the rocks.

On the way back to the main road we noticed that a water tank on the rear of a converted bus, parked just off the side of the track, was leaking. There were lights in the bus so we stopped to inform the owner about his leak. He knew, but he offered us a beer anyway. Barry was the chief buyer for the Goldsworthy Mining Group and he was on holidays with his family. Buoyed by the beers we had swallowed, the comfort of sitting in quite luxurious lounge chairs in Barry's bus and the good company we pressed on into a night of considerable difficulty. Rain was teeming down in great drops and it was getting late.

It was well after midnight when we arrived at Sandfire and despite the rain there were several citizens lying around the building, asleep. We needed petrol so we knocked loudly. Finally a short tempered man, with very heavy forearms, came out to tell us that the bar was shut and to piss off. We told him we wanted to see Eddie Norton. He asked why. We told him that Barry had sent us. That was the key. He not only filled our tank he also invited us into the bar where a few hardy stayers were still enjoying each other's company. There we enjoyed several shots of Scotch whisky and riotous bush stories.

Finally we left and proceeded in the rain on a diabolical road with huge corrugations, many washaways, and with vast puddles that splashed muddy water over the windscreen as we charged through. During the night we came across many vehicles either bogged or pulled over to the side of the road, unable to continue. We finally arrived at the turn off to Broome, where there is now a service station called Roebuck but which was only bare road at that time, at first light and punctured immediately we hit our first patch of bitumen. This required us to drag a spare tyre off the roof rack and change the bloody thing when we were so tired we could hardly stand up. We were the last car through for a week. This time the Port Hedland to Sandfire leg, on a bitumen road in fine weather was easy.

At Sandfire, where we stopped for sandwiches, Nick and I exchanged seats. I had covered the best part of 600km and I had hogged the bike for the whole trip up till then. I forgave myself my selfishness on the basis that, as I explained to my sons, it was my last ride. Nonetheless Nick wanted a ride, and I think he was secretly concerned about my stamina, so he had the pleasure of two wheels for the 320 odd kilometres to Broome, another very easy leg.

We drove in to the growing town of Broome, in tandem, late in the afternoon. There was no accommodation of any kind, available anywhere. Given that Broome is a tourist town we had not bothered to book and we found it difficult to believe there was no room at the inn. There had never been any problem on any other trip. Eventually we found a caravan park that had a bit of room on their car park so we set up the tents for the first time. We had trouble unhitching the trailer. One of the shackles had become twisted and we could not undo it. After a fair bit of effort and by using blasphemy as a lubricant we managed to get things undone but we needed new shackles.

After this poor start we got out the folding table with its attached chairs and the folding camp chairs and set the whole lot up. My camp chair is a very fancy affair with a recess in the arm rest that will accommodate a stubby. It rejoices in the title "Monarch". There was a minor concern when we found that the air mattresses were deflating even though we had checked them before we left Perth and we became a bit gloomy because things were not going well. After several cold beers out of our ice box and after the boys had chatted to the Swedish birds in the next tent we felt relaxed and were not too concerned about paltry matters such as twisted shackles and deflating mattresses.

I should have concerned myself more about the air mattress having seen Cyril White chasing his deflating mattress around in the moonlight on Cable Beach a long time ago, after several hours in the "Conti" pub, and eventually doing it to death with an entrenching tool. Deflating mattresses are no joke to hard bitten Aussie travellers. We need ice cold beer, good sleeping bags and air mattresses or we sulk.

Feeling expansive after our cold beers and the pleasant sights of numerous scantily clad, young, nubile, Scandinavian ladies running around we found our way to a restaurant named Frangipanis where we indulged in pasta and red wine. When we returned no one was in pain so Hans got into our tent onto the flat mattress and Nick into his. Being older and having some background in these matters I crawled into the back seat of the Range Rover where I spent a fairly uncomfortable night crunched into the foetal position with my head jammed against an arm rest. New air mattresses were going to be the first item on the agenda tomorrow.

Chapter 28.
Day 5. Wednesday July 20.
Broome to Halls Creek.

Up until yesterday all had been going to plan and then we had trouble with shackles and the air mattresses. Today the wheels fell off properly. I went out on the motorcycle fairly early to find somewhere we could buy replacement gear and found a camping store that was a bit out of town by talking to a passer by who was a fountain of information.

At 9am, when we knew the store would be open, we drove over to it and bought new mattresses and shackles. Wanting to be sure I bought a packet of the strongest shackles they had available. When we opened the packet they proved to be large enough to have restrained the "Mesopotamia" so we had to change them. We messed about putting the new shackles on, buying ice and generally getting ready. We left a little later than we should have as we had to cover about 700km to get to Halls Creek. We drove to the Roebuck turn off to fill the petrol tanks and have breakfast. The weather was good so we set off in reasonable spirits with Hans driving and me travelling behind sedately on the bike.

About 70km out of Broome a new, white Nissan Patrol passed me and then passed the boys who were obeying the speed limit. Having passed the

Range Rover the Patrol then slowed down to below the speed limit so Hans accelerated to pass it. As he got along side the bloody thing accelerated so that by the time he got past he was doing 150kph. He then returned to the speed limit and the Nissan stayed on top of the Range Rover. I was getting angry with this performance and was considering squirting past both when the Patrol again passed the Range Rover, put a blue light on the roof and pulled the boys over.

It was the Road Patrol who had found that our trailer, the trailer that had been specially prepared for the trip, had not been licensed for 10 years, the period since we had moved to Roleystone. Obviously the renewal had become lost in the post and as we were not using the trailer I did not notice the license had expired.

It had to be re-registered as soon as possible, because there was no third party cover for it, and that required a return to Broome. We agreed that I would ride on to Halls Creek where we had a motel room booked for the night and nail it down, and the boys would go back to Broome, get the trailer registered and join me late that night at the motel.

Mr. Plod, in the form of the Road Patrol does his duty and apprehends the miscreants.

I rode the rest of the 394km to Fitzroy Crossing fairly sedately in a concerned frame of mind. What would happen if the boys had an accident? How would the police view a trailer with a license that was ten years out of date and that had obviously been towed up from Perth? My mobile telephone worked at the Crossing so I contacted Nick. Things were not going well. There were problems with chassis numbers that had been painted over when the trailer was refurbished and there were not enough reflectors so they had to buy and mount some new ones. They hoped to get out of Broome by 4pm and that meant arriving at Halls Creek at about 11 that night after taking turns at driving.

I had problems of my own. There was nearly 300km to cover to Halls Creek and it was already 2.30pm. I had no ambition to be on the road at sundown. Judging by the dead kangaroo and cattle carcasses I had already passed the road was likely to become dangerous as the day wore on. I was faced with two options. I could either ride sedately, which would see me still on the road at sunset with the perils that entailed, or I could speed up and break the law. I decided that as I would rather break the law than my neck I would turn the wick up.

I scuttled along at 140-160kmh with occasional forays to 180 on straight stretches when it was clear both sides. I was nervous and there were groups of cattle at fairly regular intervals so I had to slow down frequently. I also slowed down for several of the red termite mounds that looked very much like cow's behinds and for any vehicle that I saw in the distance that looked as though it could be authority. About half way to Halls Creek the temperature dropped and I wrestled with the zips on my jacket as I tore along to close the vents but even though I managed to close them I was cold by the time I arrived. It was a potentially good ride spoiled by concern and haste.

As soon as I was in range at Halls Creek I rang the boys. They had not been able to finalize the inspection and would not be able to leave until the next day. They did not seem unduly perturbed. Later I found out that they had managed to book a highly expensive hotel room and they were looking forward to doing their laundry and a night of debauchery without their disapproving elder. Half their luck!

I was stuck at Halls Creek without a change of underclothing or a toothbrush. I downgraded from the family suite we had booked to Room 4 in the "Hollywood" area, which consists of single person rooms in transportables set in a rectangle with a barbecue at its centre.

"Hollywood" deserves a bit of space in this chronicle. The rooms are small, strictly utilitarian and always remarkably neat when you first walk into them. There is some hanging space for clothes, a narrow bed and a toilet/ shower/ basin area with a door for privacy. Oh! By the way there is also an air conditioning unit set in the end wall and the obligatory, these days, television set. The walls are tastefully finished in a mid brown fibre board that disguises some of the sins of inadequate cleaning and does not prevent noise from penetrating from one room to the next.

Hollywood was inhabited by tough men who work hard from early morning to late afternoon. When they get back to their caves they clean up and then sit around the barbecue and monosyllabically discuss the events of the day as they partake of their choice of nerve palliatives until they bed at an early hour. They were not too thrilled to see an ancient biker park his machine in the alley behind their domain for safety and invade their private space. I was obviously not one of them.

In different circumstances I might have grabbed a beer and taken it out to join them, but I was tired and the effort was beyond me. I have found that if you do make the effort you are rewarded. They are the salt of the earth and they have always forgiven me for not being one of them in the past. When I had wearily settled in I showered and ventured into the bar for a beer. The licensee and his wife were nice people so I stuck around for a meal at "Russian Jacks" restaurant and a couple more beers. At 8.30 I left "Russian Jacks" wandered back to "Hollywood", nodded to the few men still sitting in the courtyard in a haze of strange smelling smoke, who nodded back unenthusiastically, and retired for the night.

Chapter 29.
Day 6. Thursday July 21.
Halls Creek – All Day.

Thursday was spent waiting in the Halls Creek metropolis for my oldest and my youngest sons to catch up. It was not a memorable day. I arose reasonably early because I am used to waking at an early hour. I have habits similar to those once described to me by Multiplex's John Roberts as his "chook" syndrome. That is, he started to feel tired when the sun went down and awoke just before it came up.

I had a shower and then wandered into the town where I found a bakery open so I bought a pie for breakfast. Now I can hear any optimistic reader who has penetrated this far waiting for something better mutter "For God's sake – why on earth did he bother to let us know that?" If that is the way you feel please go back to the first page of this essay. You were warned.

I then scoured the limited library at the motel and found a book with the name "Billy Sunday" as its title and returned to my room on the courtyard of "Hollywood", which still had the foreign aroma of odd burnt substances from the previous evening, and I do not mean the barbecue. "Billy Sunday" is an American story set in the 1860s and it is surreal. It was about the trials of the early settlers (invaders?) and their interface with the indigenous people, especially the interface – if that is the word – of white men and Red Indian women.

At mid afternoon feeling thoroughly drowsy from lying around reading I moved into a family room and waited. Just after 5pm the boys turned up, much to my relief. We did some washing in the laundrette and settled into our quarters. There was a bit of drama when the Road Patrol turned up but they were not after us for a change. Then we became concerned that they were there to invade the "Hollywood" crowd and whatever illegal activities they might be getting up to. We were right, they were there for the Hollywood crowd – they joined them.

After some nerve settlers we wandered into "Russian Jacks" for barramundi and more beers. We bedded early in a mellow mood and with optimism about tomorrow.

Chapter 30.
Day 7. Friday July 22.
Halls Creek to Purnululu.

We arose early, paid our bill and left for Warmun, just over 160km away. It was to prove to be a big day with some wonderful scenes. The ride to Warmun was marred by the V4 Honda performing poorly. It was well down on power and, it turned out later, it swallowed a great deal more fuel than it normally did. Because the bike was sluggish and I was concerned about the plethora of road kill I travelled slowly behind the Range Rover. The riding conditions did not require much concentration and my mind wandered.

On each dead kangaroo I passed there were either eagles or crows and my first thought was - what did all these carrion eaters dine on before there were the easy pickings of road kill? How has the road and the traffic on it affected the balance of nature?

Then, for no apparent reason, I asked myself why the human race was so obsessed with striking spheres and ovoids with precision? They come in a variety of shapes, solidities and sizes these "balls". Some are hollow and light. Some are small and dense. Some are propelled by feet or other body parts and some by racquets, bats and clubs of wondrous shape that are highly technological. This strange obsession of the human specie I do not understand although I have shared it and I would have been delighted to have been a champion cricketer, footballer, hockey player, tennis star or golfer but even sharing the obsession I do not understand why we have it. Why have games assumed the importance they have? What is the driving force behind the obsession? How can otherwise intelligent humans spend the best years of their lives devoted to forcing a sphere or ovoid to go where they want it to go? Will I ever understand why there is such an obsession? Perhaps it is better to let games remain a mystery and just enjoy them.

With many of the wonders of the world understanding can reduce enjoyment. There is no sauce as piquant as the flavouring of the unknown. Professionals in any sphere have to understand what makes what happens in that sphere – be it music, architecture, sport, physics, chemistry, engineering, mathematics, agriculture, finance, the human body, whatever – but in the very act of gaining this knowledge there is a loss of the magic that comes from ignorance. When we finally know everything there is to know will there be any magic left?

Once at Warmun I left the motorcycle in an enclosure that is there to safely hold vehicles that are temporarily not needed and we all trooped off to have toasted sandwiches for breakfast. I know that that piece of information is not exactly riveting but I want the reader to realize just what some of the hardships of long distance travel are all about, and toasted sandwiches from Warmun are a definite hardship. They are not in the top ten on anybody's list of good grub and even a starving Ethiopian would be tempted to give one a miss. At Warmun, probably in an endeavour to maximise our enjoyment of them, they made us wait 55 minutes for the sandwiches. When we enquired politely as to what was happening, after others had come and gone away with their mouths full, they suddenly realized that our order had disappeared. If the late delivery was a ploy to increase our enjoyment of the food it failed.

Nick, Hans and I all left Warmun in the Range Rover and headed back towards Halls Creek until we arrived at the Purnululu turn off. Purnululu Park has within it those wonders of nature, the Bungle Bungles. The drive in to the Bungle Bungles is on a reasonable gravel road that twists and turns across the plain and between hills. It is a drive with interest and a good precursor to the wonders of the park itself.

When we reached the tourist centre we paid our dues and received a map of the park in return. We opted for one of the camping areas and dropped the

The walk into Echidna Chasm.

A bower bird's nest near the path on the walk into Echidna Chasm.

The old man and his youngest offspring. Unfortunately the flash has washed out much of the colour of the chasm.

trailer off there. Then we headed for Echidna Chasm. I had never heard of it. It is magnificent. The walk in is well worthwhile with its palms and red hills on each side. There is even a bower bird's nest.

The crack in the red stone that is the chasm is startling. It is only 1m wide in places and it is over 150m high.

We walked up the chasm as far as we could go - several hundred metres. It is quite an experience and it reminded me of parts of Hancock Gorge in the Karajini Park, but Hancock Gorge is even more terrific and it has water flowing through it. On the drive to the chasm we had seen a ridge of rock near the track that looked interesting so we decided to climb it on the way back. The boys climbed with dash and élan and I climbed with much panting and determination. Photographs were taken and the wonderful vistas admired, while I caught my breath.

We descended and on the way down decided, urged on by Nick, that we would hang the expense and take a helicopter ride over the Bungle Bungles. This involved driving 28km to the airstrip over reasonable roads, which we covered in quick time but we were still too late for the last circuit of the day. They stopped at 4pm.

There is spectacular scenery everywhere you look around the Purnululu Park.

We booked for the first flight Saturday morning and we drove further north as the sun set and the colours changed. There are wonderfully shaped rocks, slender buttes and incredibly coloured and layered cliff faces wherever you look, some of them now turning a hazy purple and some still glowing a radiant orange in the light of the setting sun.

We went as far as we could before the light gave out and then turned and headed for the camping site over the winding, corrugated road.

We set up our tents, blew up our new air mattresses, which stayed up, even after I drove over one, cooked a meal over the gas camp stove and settled down with a G&T for me and icy beers from the ice box for the boys. Then we broke out the shower bucket, threw a rope over a tree branch and showered. Chilly, bracing stuff in falling temperatures but we all felt better after. The temperature fell further as the boys played cards and I made notes. We retired fairly early. It was a cool night in central Australia. It had been a great day and even better was promised for tomorrow.

Chapter 31.
Day 8. Saturday July 23.
Purnululu to Kununurra.

Today Kaye and Nick's wife Rachel were due to arrive in Kununurra by air so we had an appointment for which only a crisis such as asphyxiation through strangulation by a demon python or being eaten by blood crazed kangaroos would be regarded as a reasonable excuse if we failed to be there to pick them up - and even death would be accepted only grudgingly as an excuse.

We broke camp at 5.30am. Each re-packing of a full trailer is a new challenge and today it was made more difficult because we had to get as much out of the Range Rover and into the trailer as possible in case we had to go directly to the airport to pick up the ladies. We arrived at the helicopter pad with the fully laden trailer in tow at 7.30, mingled with the other passengers, paid the price of admission and had a cup of coffee. At precisely 8.00am the three helicopters started to take off.

Our larger and slightly slower craft was to be tail end Charlie. It was piloted by Neville from Newcastle who had only been in the area the standard 3 weeks. I say standard because that seemed to be the reply we received whenever we asked how long anyone had been where they were. There is obviously a very large floating population moving on at three weekly intervals.

Because of his newness Neville was not the greatest fount of information on the area but he was a careful and obviously competent flier and he was a nice bloke. Conditions were calm and the light was terrific. We flew over Y Gorge, Cathedral Gorge, the Fingers, the Horseshoe Plain, Piccaninny Gorge, the Domes and the formation known as the Coalition. No description of the shapes, colours, variations, light, vegetation and striations can give you an adequate idea of the visual impact of the area nor do photographs give a true indication of the stately grandeur of the area. The flight was an exciting half hour that was, unfortunately, over in what seemed to be only a few minutes. Many photographs, and a bit of video, were taken.

The Bungle Bungles. To understand their true grandeur and ambience you have to be there.

Photographs do not convey the true majesty.

We scuttled off back to Warmun as soon as we landed, satisfied that our money had been well spent. Time appeared to now be a problem that later events showed it was not. Once at Warmun I retrieved the VFR and we ingested a hamburger. I do not recommend that town as a stopping point on any gourmet tour you decide to take through the north.

As I reported earlier the Honda had performed very poorly on the tank full of juice I bought at Halls Creek. It would not go faster than 130kmh, it lacked power and it chewed through the tank full in record time. Maybe I received the dregs of something not quite kosher from the service station when I filled the tank at the Creek. During the filling process I was pestered by two bright eyed little boys who tried my helmet on and begged for a ride. I felt I was being a real mean bastard because I would not oblige them but I was concerned as to what their elders might have thought and, anyway, I did not have a spare helmet. They were appealing kids. Why do such appealing young turn into the shambling wrecks their elders so often are?

After that little detour I shall return to the bike at Warmun. In an attempt to get performance back I bought a canister of injector fluid (yes the V4 is injected) and poured the recommended dosage into the bike's tank before filling up. The rest went into the Range Rover. Voila! – a return of performance and the best use of fuel of the trip. The elixir had worked.

The 200km to Kununurra were covered in less than 2 hours and we still had some time so we checked in to the apartment block Nick had booked, parked and locked up the trailer, emptied the car and we even had time to hose it down, which it desperately needed. Then we showered and shaved. We were going easy. Nick rang the airport to find out just what time the plane was going to land and found out it had already landed – early. We scuttled out to the airport and were there in time to receive the women who were our two wives and one mother. After the ladies settled in we had a rest and later devoted time to shopping for food and having a look at the town. We ate our first meal together at the Kununurra Tavern and retired early. It had been a big day.

Chapter 32.
Day 9. July 24.
Around Kununurra.

We all arose in a leisurely fashion at 7.30. Kaye produced fruit salad and the well known Australian breakfast of "bake neggs". We set out to wander with 5 of us crammed into the Range. We travelled over the green and irrigated Packsaddle Plains. We climbed Kelly's Knob and took photographs. We visited the ford at Ivanhoe Crossing and paddled on its slippery surface. We tried the locally made booze at The Hoochery. We visited a couple of rock galleries where we admired Zebra Stone and other wonders and we fed the catfish in Lake Kununurra. We trundled around enjoying the ambience, each other's company and the sense of freedom that comes when you are on holiday and there are no immediate commitments. After a siesta we had a barbecue beside the pool at Lakeside Villas, which was our temporary home. We had a couple of drinks and played cards. It was a thoroughly pleasant and unhurried day.

Chapter 33.
Day 10. July 25.
Kununurra to El Questro.

The hardest part of leaving Kununurra was finding a place to leave the Honda V4 in safety. The roads out to El Questro, part of which is the notorious Gibb River Road, are not recommended for heavy road bikes and my sense of adventure has been tempered by age and experience. I had no ambition to damage the bike and leave parts of my epidermis and the bike's panelling on unrideable roads.

As it turned out the roads to El Questro were rideable and I could have taken it. The local BP garage, from whom we had purchased large quantities of fuel, found they did not have room for it (?) and suggested I try a storage facility at 13 Poinciana Road. They kindly drew up a map that led me, with the Range Rover in tow, to Poinsettia Road. Poinsettia Road is a loop and the Range and I did several laps of it without finding anything that looked like a storage facility or finding number 13. Nick made enquiries at number 15 where the guard dog bit him. When he finally got past the beast he received the standard reply for this part of the world – "Don't know mate. I have only been here 3 weeks myself".

A flash of inspiration occurred and Nick and I studied the town map and there, sure enough, was a Poinciana Road, some distance away. After several cries of "I knew I had seen the name before" from our incredibly erudite lot we repaired there. Because in Kununurra everyone knows where everything is numbers are not given a high priority and I was still having trouble finding the storage unit when I saw a large shed with BGC emblazoned on it. The man inside, Peter O'S was charming and after finding out that I knew Len Buckeridge, the B of BGC (the GC stands for Group of Companies), he let me put the bike safely inside his shed. I tucked it up lovingly and covered it. Then we all took off for El Questro.

It is quite a trip. Once you leave the bitumen there are grey roads that smoke behind vehicles. However the Gibb River Road on which we had to travel for some distance was not the fearsome beast that Paul Bennett and I and later Kaye, Nick, Hans and I had travelled on years ago. The road skirts the picturesque Cockburn Range so the scenery is good.

We found the road into El Questro was not a highway but it is not the worst road in WA either. On the way in we pulled into Zebedee Springs. It is a wonderland of warm pools, small waterfalls, palms – Livingstonia, Pandanus and wonderful palms that grow in a helix and are locally called Corkscrew Palms - white stemmed eucalypts, sheer orange-red stone cliffs, lush growth and dappled sunlight. The naked ape was disporting various specimens of itself in the pools. It was shortly before noon and the place was packed.

A sign said "Zebedee Springs must be vacated by noon". Kaye asked a ranger why that was and received the surprising answer that after 12 the tourist buses arrived and the pools became too crowded. As it already looked a bit like the Tokyo underground at 5 o'clock we decided to leave and to come back out of rush hour.

At El Questro we were directed to out tents for night one and dumped our gear. Then we wandered down to "The Old Swimming Hole". The rope on which naked apes with more energy than sense can swing out over the swimming hole so they can fall at ungainly angles into the pool and splash more sedate and refined people who are enjoying the bush ambience and quietly reading was, thankfully, up a tree and out of reach. Naturally enough Hans retrieved it at risk of life and limb and then he, Rachel and Nick, with loud and unseemly noises issuing from them, swung out over the tranquil pool and completely ruined its peace. Still – it tires the children out and they sleep well.

At 5pm Nick and I went up to the kiosk/tavern and booked a trip for all of us for Wednesday morning, on the boat that takes gawkers up Chamberlain Gorge. Having accomplished this difficult feat we thought that we were entitled to a reward so we sat under a tree with nice cold cans of beer and had a yarn. When we decided we had been there long enough to have made ourselves unpopular but not so long that we would be completely ostracized we wandered back to tent land and got cleaned up and changed. Then the whole lot of us returned to the Tavern at sunset. Kaye and I watched a slide show of the place and its people and at 6.30 we went to dinner at the restaurant. The food and wine were excellent and the bill was substantial. Back to bed in our insect proof tents at a reasonable hour.

Hans displaying some youthful exuberance at the El Questro swimming hole.

Chapter 34.
Day 11. July 26.
Around El Questro.

Today we moved into two bungalows and we had to vacate our tents by 10am so we packed our gear into the trailer early and went back to Zebedee Springs, leaving the trailer at the camp site. This time the beauty of the place was just as great but the pools were not so clogged with bodies. The young enjoyed sitting under the waterfalls but Kaye and I found the water cloyingly warm. After the juvenile delinquents had had their fill of soaking, they were becoming waterlogged and the crowd was thickening, we decided to go to El Questro Gorge. As we wandered back to the car a guide pointed to Nick and Rachel, who were in top form, and told his gang of followers "Do you know, when that pair came in they were eighty four years old?"

El Questro Gorge is also wonderful, maybe even more wonderful depending on your taste. It has a stream flowing through it which is so clear that it is only by the surface sheen, the slightly darker colouring of the stones under the surface and the distortion of diffraction an observer can discern there is a stream at all. On both sides there are towering, vertical cliffs some areas of which are covered in the largest and most lush fishtail ferns I have ever seen.

There are large, surreally shaped gum trees and more beautiful palms. The path wanders through this wonderland and we followed it enjoying every moment until, 1.3km from the parking area, we reached a large boulder that completely filled the gorge and had at its base a water hole of cool, diamond clear water that simply begged to be swum in. The rock was passable and earlier in my career I certainly would have scaled it and hungrily devoured the rest of the gorge.

Beautiful El Questro Gorge, the vegetation is lush and the water sparklingly clear.

This time I was content to enjoy where I was with Kaye while Nick and Hans went on. The pool already had people in it and sitting around its edges in dappled sunlight so I joined them. If you are looking for a solitary existence El Questro gorge is not the place to go in winter.

We left because our barometer of the state of our food intake, Hans's hunger pains, was telling us it was time for lunch. Even Nick, not normally given to excess and quite stoical by nature, was heard to mutter that he was hungry enough to eat the crotch out of a low flying duck. The walk back to the camping area was every bit as good as the walk in. Back at the camp we found that out bungalows were ready for occupation so we moved in and ate. Kaye and Rachel made an impressive pile of sandwiches that disappeared quickly and we sat on our veranda looking down at the stream passing by amid Pandanus palms and large and twisted Paper Barks. Peace and tranquillity reigned. But not for long. After a rest Hans, Nick and I played cards competitively and noisily and drank a good deal of beer. As the beer disappeared the competition became more intense and the noise volume rose. At sundown we went back to the restaurant, ate a fulfilling meal and polished off a bottle of good red. A great day ended in quiet contentment.

Another view of stunning El Questro Gorge. Just look at the clarity of that water.

Chapter 35.
Day 12. July 27.
More El Questro and then Argyle.

This morning we, and a crowd of other gawkers, trooped over to Chamberlain Gorge where a boat, its crew and a guide awaited us. The gorge is filled for three kilometres, at this time of the year, with fresh, clear water. With its ancient stone walls it is beautiful and it has a long history.

Part of its recent history is that a couple were in a small boat, fishing on the serene waters between the orange bluffs, when their craft was attacked by a salt water crocodile trapped in the fresh water lake. Their gear fell out one side and they fell out the other. They made the shore while the croc' was engaged with the bait but both were badly frightened. Our guide, Snaf, (don't ask), advised against swimming and told us that if the boat did founder we were to throw the food and the skipper out one side and swim for the shore on the other.

The boat took us up the gorge as far as it could go and we pulled in against a flat rock. On the way up rock wallabies were enticed out to entertain us. It turns out they like chook pellets. These beautiful little creatures, who are quite at home on sheer cliffs, are slowly being wiped out by feral foxes. I think there are good reasons why it would be better to wipe out the feral foxes.

Peaceful Chamberlain Gorge has many attractions but saltwater crocodiles have been known to inhabit it so swimming is not recommended.

Another view of Chamberlain Gorge near the area we disembarked.

After we had disembarked, which is a technical term meaning that we got off the boat, we were led up the gorge a short way and given a dissertation on Aboriginal Wandjina and Bradshaw art. The Bradshaw figures are a good deal older than the Wandjina figures and they appear to be more sophisticated so there is a theory that they were made by inhabitants who lived in the area before the arrival of the Aborigines. This unprovable theory is not popular with some of those of Aboriginal background, who now gain financial benefits, if no other benefits, from, if the theory is true, the even more recent white invaders. To cut a long story down to a manageable size the guides are now no longer permitted to point out the painted figures in the gorge. I guess having them subjected to the searching gaze of tourists wears them out. They were only permitted to tell us about them. By the sheerest coincidence we tourists noticed that there were Wandjina figures on the cliff face almost immediately above the guide telling us about them *(see photo below)*. We were incredibly lucky that he had selected that particular flat rock to sit on while he told us about the art.

The intrepid Bruechles went exploring and Nick found Bradshaw figures further up the gorge. They were duly photographed. If you are not familiar with Bradshaw figures you should find out about them. They are an artistic and very elegant tour de force. The gorge is also home to some beautiful native plants in a wonderful setting. It is a marvellous place for which photographs cannot do justice. Then we boated back to our vehicles. If ever you are at El Questro you must take the expedition to Chamberlain Gorge. Not only will you get the benefit of the beauties of the gorge, the wildlife, the plant life and the art, you will also get the benefit of a fresh and nutritious lunch served on the boat and some entertaining stories.

Wandjina paintings in Chamberlain Gorge. Note the tiny, much older, Bradshaw figure near the bottom left hand corner.

The many stemmed Durack Tree – an ancient Boab.

Beautiful, peaceful and grand though it was we were not satiated by the gorge and we were running out of time at El Questro so we set off for Branco's Lookout. The road needs a 4 wheel drive and entails several fairly rough patches and a couple of creek crossings. You pass what is known as the Durack Tree, an ancient, many stemmed boab into which a variety of clowns have carved their names.

The Lookout reveals a sensational vista. Even El Questro Homestead can be seen. You are only allowed to go to the Homestead if you are Kylie Minogue or someone of equal stature and importance to the development of humankind.

Apart from being jolted around the trip is great. The streams, the bush, the wildflowers and the land are appealing. It was all a bit rushed but it had to be because we still had a long way to go.

The view from Branco's Lookout.

We returned to the bungalows and packed the trailer, which was not easy as we now had two extra bodies and their gear to deal with. We paid our bills and set off in the crowded Range Rover over the mediocre roads. Our cramped conditions were somewhat alleviated by the views of the Cockburn Range that were spread out on the left hand side for our approval.

At Kununurra we retrieved the bike from BGC, filled tanks and headed for Argyle. Nick had been sitting crammed between two bodies in the rear of the Range from El Questro to Kununurra and wanted freedom. He put in an order for the ride on the motorcycle to Argyle and, stricken with conscience over my selfishness to that time, I did not have the heart to deny him the pleasure of the ride there. Rachel also thought that a ride in the breeze would be refreshing so she elected to ride pillion.

Suddenly we had room to burn in the Range Rover. Kaye drove and Hans spreadeagled himself on the rear seat. The drive to Argyle, once you leave the main highway, is quite marvellous. A good road winds between hills. The Kapok trees were in full, golden bloom. Occasional termite mounds and trees dotted the Spinifex covered hills over which there had been fires in the fairly recent past. The effect was not unlike a Fred Williams landscape.

After what seemed to be a very short period we were there and we were delighted to find that our accommodation was brand new and perched on the edge of the cliff looking over Lake Argyle. The lake's surface, backed by rolling hills that were in bright sunlight, lay darkly shadowed below our feet. A beautiful and comfortable place it was and we knew we were going to enjoy our stay there. The bungalow had several bedrooms, a well equipped kitchen, a couple of bathrooms and a wide veranda poised on the edge of the drop down to the lake. On the veranda there was that great Australian necessity – a gas heated barbecue. It was a million dollar location and it was, temporarily, all ours. A hundred metres away was the centre of town – a bar cum shop cum restaurant – just over the only piece of lawn in town. Perfection!

Million dollar views from the deck in our "front yard" at Argyle.

Near sundown, with the tops of the hills surrounding the lake still brightly lit but Lake Argyle itself in shadow, we drove down to its edge and threw lines into the dark surface from a floating jetty. Hans immediately caught a good size catfish that we returned relatively unscathed. Then Nick's bait was taken by something that was so big he was having difficulty holding it on the nylon line. Eventually it bit through a substantial hook. Several more catfish were landed and returned but Nick's monster did not reappear.

Rachel with a catfish against the darkening lake with the hills in the background still in bright light.

Right on sunset boats arrived on trailers. We chatted to a couple of the locals in charge of the boats while they waited for their passengers to arrive. We found out that Argyle was the best place in the world to live and that the water was so free of contaminants that when you washed your car you just let it dry, and it dried in a perfectly clean state.

As the sun set the boats and their passengers took off across the still, dark surface into the deepening gloom trailing ever widening ripples. The scene of boats, dark water and rolling hills in bright sunlight had a sense of deep peace about it. None of us wanted to leave but driven by the very human lust not to miss anything we drove to the dam wall, crossed it on the road that has been built on its crest, and then entered the park at the bottom of the wall. We walked around the park admiring it and listening to the roar of the water that passes through discharge pipes and drives turbines that produce electrical power, and then follows the old Ord river bed to be held up by the wall that creates Lake Kununurra, the source of the water for the irrigated areas. As it grew dark we turned for home.

This picture from above the dam wall gives some idea of the tranquillity of the lake on a winter afternoon but it does not give any idea of the scale of the body of water.

I do not possess the skills necessary to convey how remarkably beautiful and timeless the scenery of Australia is. Let your imagination fill in the gaps that I leave. The photographs will give you some idea but they cannot convey the scale or the peace of a place such as Lake Argyle as the sun sets.

I cooked a "hash and mash" with fresh ingredients we had bought in Kununurra and, replete, we watched the news on satellite TV and retired early to bed to read. Another wonderful and full day had been lived.

The roar of the water as it passes through the discharge pipes is quite something.

Chapter 36.
Day 13. July 28.
At Argyle.

Today was Thursday and time was running out. Our wives had to be back at Kununurra on Saturday. We arose at 6.30am, ate a light breakfast and did some laundry. Today we were to go boating on the Lake for the first time.

In the several visits that I, together with Nick and others, have made to Argyle previously I had never been out on the lake. I have always in too much of a tearing hurry to get to somewhere else. Today was to be a new experience for everyone, including me. We walked the short distance to the tavern and boarded a bus that took us down to the boat ramp from which we had fished the previous evening.

The boat we boarded was a flat bottomed affair that planed fairly easily on the calm surface of the lake, with a Sarlon canopy that protected passengers from the bright sun. It skimmed out into the lake and stopped at places of interest such as the dam wall, and the excavation from which the rock for the dam wall was taken by means of a "coyote" series of explosive blasts. The valley left by the excavation now serves as an alternate spillway in the event of the dam being in danger of overtopping.

We paused at islands on which there were various colonies of birds, freshwater crocodiles sunning themselves and large spiders spinning their

The bird life around the lake is abundant and varied.

webs in stubby trees. We were informed that these webs were "the strongest in the world". Our guide told us that the Yanks had taken samples of web back to the good old US of A, had analysed the material and were now synthesising it for "peaceful purposes", such as bullet proof vests. We have much to be thankful to nature for.

The boat was stopped in a bay and pieces of bread were dangled over the side. Archer fish accurately shot the pieces with jets of water so that they then fell soggily into the lake where they were scooped up by catfish and barramundi. There is an abundance of fish life, especially catfish, in the lake and there are many Johnson River freshwater crocodiles to eat them.

One element that was pointed out to us during our tour was the remains of a barramundi farm that was poised to make a great deal of money but which was wiped out by the cyclone Ingrid a couple of years before. The life cycle of the barramundi was then given an airing. They all start life in fresh water and they are all male. Then they make their way out into the ocean where they grow bigger and better and some change to female. They then make their way back to their original habitat to breed and the cycle starts again. Because of the dam wall the barra' in Lake Argyle cannot run away to sea so the whole 400 tonnes in the fish farm were male and this was not desirable, because all male barra' that have never been to sea do not have the taste and texture of barra' that have. Several sailors I know would agree with these sentiments – seamen are superior and some turn into girls once out in a terrifyingly stormy sea. There was an attempt to ship the barra' to Queensland but concerns about genetic differences were raised. In the finish the whole lot went for cray bait. Then the cyclone destroyed the farm. Another burst dream. What we did not find out was what was going to happen to the barra' in the lake as they cannot breed. Maybe they will die out.

This little fellow is a rock wallaby.

We wandered about parts of the placid 1000 square kilometre lake between its surround of rounded ancient hills and while we did we were provided with important statistics. For instance, when the lake is full to the brim, as it was when cyclone Ingrid passed through, it has a capacity 67 times that of Sydney Harbour and contains about one sixth of all of Australia's fresh water. Most of the time its capacity is about 35 "Sydharbs". The dam wall was not designed to be overtopped. If overtopping occurred the wall would be destroyed and the citizens of Kununurra would have good reasons for heading to higher ground. Therefore there are several escape routes for the excess water, one of them being the valley left by the removal of material for the wall, mentioned previously.

Other figures that were given to us were that the hydro-electric power station at the dam wall's base provides all the power for Argyle, Kununurra and Wyndham and, probably of greater importance, for the Argyle Diamond Mine. The mine workings are now completely "green" whereas previously they used millions of litres of diesel. In the production of this power the dam level falls by 6mm each day. This compares quite favourably with evaporation from the surface, which is about 14mm per day. And the water used for power is not wasted. As I reported earlier it flows down to the pipe head dam in the ancient Ord river bed where it becomes Lake Kununurra and where it is used for irrigation of the Kununurra food bowl.

There is no doubt that Lake Argyle is a major Australian asset and it is an asset the full value of which we have not yet seen. We should thank the vision of those who conceived it. There is also no doubt that the lake has a unique ambience, set as it is among rolling hills covered in the ubiquitous Spinifex, with its bird life and its fish and crocodiles.

Such a vast oasis set in a desert has an appeal all its own. I would be happy to spend a couple of months exploring it. Perhaps Australia should be considering other, similar oases across northern Australia, where good monsoonal rains fall in summer, to create food bowls for a world that will surely not have enough if the present population growth continues.

However Lake Argyle is not unalloyed joy. It now covers the birth places and sacred sites of many indigenous people, who regret their loss. It also covers the sheds and equipment of the Durack family who pioneered the area for the white settlers. Their house was saved and moved to higher ground where it serves as a museum for tourists, of which Kaye and I were later to be two, but the station buildings were inundated by waters that rose more quickly than had been estimated.

A Durack, Michael, superintends the old homestead. He is a man who does not believe in basking in past glories. An hour or two spent with Michael and the Durack house is time well spent. Looking at the Durack house shows you how easy life has become since his forebears first drove their cattle over from Queensland. Is life now too easy? Do we now have the courage and the capabilities that would enable us to accept the challenges that these brave people once undertook? Were these pioneers heroic, as I believe they were, or were they despoilers of a paradise, as many others appear to believe?

At the end of our boat trip we wended our way to our hill top bungalow and had a siesta. Rachel and Nick took off on the V4 and Kaye and I followed them a short time later in the Range Rover. We visited the Durack house, drove to lookout points and later drove, again, to the park at the bottom of the dam wall while the sun set. We rounded out the day sitting on our veranda above the lake playing highly competitive and noisy card games while we drank beer. I exaggerate – the males did that, the women were much more circumspect. Dinner was a barbecue prepared with dash by Nicholas.

Durack Homestead in its new lcoation.

Chapter 37.
Day 14. July 29.
The Ord River Trip.

Today we split up. Nick and I clambered aboard the V4 and took off for Kununurra early so that we could catch the boat that travels up the Ord from there to the dam wall. Not everyone wanted to make the trip and the compromise that was decided on, after a certain amount of heartburn, was for Nick and me to take the bike to Kununurra and leave it there. We could obviously not take the Range because that would have left us with no way of getting down to Kununurra later and volunteers to drive down to Kununurra and back were conspicuously absent.

If you ever intend to make the boat journey, and after you read about it you ought to want to, do it from Kununurra and make it a return trip. It is a brilliant way of spending a day. As you already know the water flow is maintained by the water passing through the hydro electric system and it is sufficient to keep the river navigable all year round.

The ride down was done in fair time but without any heroics. We ambled along at 120kph. You see, I am haunted by the fall I had in the rain on a patch of oil when my father was riding pillion. I have had nightmares about depositing a son on the road to round out the cycle since my sons started to turn up. I do not mind trying hard when I am on my own but I am distinctly nervous when I have a passenger – especially a son.

The fruit bats rest in their trees alongside Lake Kununurra. At dusk they darken the sky they are in such numbers.

Anyway Nick and I arrived at the meeting point on time, parked the bike safely and caught the bus that was to pick up the other passengers and deliver all of us to the boat. This was a broad, low draft craft powered by, wait for it, three 200HP Honda outboard motors. That is a lot of motor. As the craft takes off the passengers are thrust back into their seats impressively. It will trundle along at what I judged to be at least 60kph.

We sat in our seats, protected from a bright sun by a fixed canopy but with the sides completely open, and we were taken out into Lake Kununurra, the lake behind the diversion dam. This lake extends from the diversion dam about two thirds of the way back to the Argyle dam.

As we trawled at low speed through the lilies on the lake's surface we were shown fruit bat colonies and various birds. These appeared to excite others aboard the craft a good deal more than they excited me. The fruit bats, hanging like bags of excreta from their home trees, were not exactly beautiful. Nor did they improve the freshness of the morning air.

Despite my lack of excitement about flying mammals and relatives of pterodactyls I found it pleasant enough sitting in my seat as the boat motored along on a fine morning. The still, dark lake is attractive with its surround of greenery, its floating water lilies and, occasionally rising from the reflective surface, stark, grey, skeletons of trees drowned when the lake was formed. We passed the only pumping station necessary for the Ord Irrigation Scheme, a station that raises the water a few metres to irrigate the Packsaddle Plains. As we quietly trawled along we saw a good deal of bird life, the heavy vegetation on each side of our water highway and the occasional fresh water crocodile.

Then the skipper applied the power and we were off. Even though the "lake" behind the diversion dam wall extends for many kilometres it is not long before the boat enters the gorge carved by the Ord, and an impressive sight it is. Red cliffs and high hills each side make it spectacular country in clear, warm air.

There are many freshwater crocodiles basking in the sun alongside the Ord River. They are a handsome relic of the past and they do not appear to like the taste of humans because no aggressive attack by one has been recorded. You must not make the mistake of confusing an aggressive "salty" for one of these relatively harmless creatures.

The glorious scenery of the Ord River.

The skipper, Cam', is an archetypal Australian. He has characteristics that most Australians would like to think are our quintessential Australian nature. He is calm, able, humorous and friendly. He handles his craft with dexterity whilst addressing his rapt audience and he has a surprising depth of knowledge of the history, geography, botany and biology of the river. He informed us that he would not go back for a hat that blew off - a likelihood given the speeds to which he took the craft - he would only go back for a body overboard. This did not mean that if you lost your hat all you had to do was to throw yourself over the side because, although he would then go back to pick you up, he would still not retrieve your head gear.

View after stunning view passed by all too quickly. We passed three Canadian canoes trolling slowly downstream. The people in them were getting a closer and more prolonged acquaintance with the river than we were. I wished I had the time to do such a trip and recalled other and more testing canoe trips such as one on the Blackwood in winter with Kaye and a three day saga on the Murchison with Ken Broadhurst when it was in flood.

The water monitor who arrived to tidy up at our luncheon stop. He was fearless and gorgeous.

Another freshwater crocodile sunning itself near the base of the dam wall.

We stopped for an excellent picnic lunch at a little bay in which a very small crocodile was making his home. He sat on the surface doing his successful best to look like a dead stick and examined the naked apes as they jumped ashore from the prow of the craft. There were tables and toilets and a shade cloth cover. Cam' refused help and laid out all the food and drinks himself. The food was fresh and excellent. As the meal neared its end a water monitor, which is a fairly large and beautiful reptile, appeared to help tidy up. It was not frightened by we tourists even when we gathered around it and thrust cameras in its face to immortalize the encounter.

After we had eaten and tidied up we re-boarded our boat and continued upstream. Cam' took us into tributaries where water-deposited debris could be seen 6m up trees. He pointed out the nest of a purple Swamp Hen well above ground level where she and her chicks had a chance of avoiding being snapped up by a hungry crocodile. What with the views, the eddying river surface, the red bluffs, the river edge greenery and the flow of information on the flora and fauna the trip was over very quickly. Then suddenly we were at the dam wall where our last act aboard was to photograph crocs lying around on rocks sun baking. Our trip was over.

We disembarked for the last time and were transported to Argyle in a bus. Nick and I left the rest of the gang to go back to our bungalow perched over the lake. They were going to be taken out on the Lake and were then going to be transported back to Kununurra in the bus. Afterwards our whole family had dinner at the tavern and then had a couple of hard fought card games at home that Hans won. Nick and I thought that the boat trip had been a marvellous experience but we did not make too much of a fuss about it. It is better not to rub salt into wounds.

Pelicans, herons, darters, cormorants and more thrive on the Ord River.

Chapter 38.
Day 15. 30 July.
Argyle to Kununurra.

Nick cooked bacon and eggs for breakfast and we packed up, with regret. The drive back through the hills to Kununurra in the cool morning air was just as enjoyable as the trip up had been, but with five bodies in the car it was more crowded. When we arrived it was still too early for us to get into our accommodation so we went to the town centre, had a snack and wandered about. We bought some fresh supplies. Rachel and Nick visited an art gallery displaying aboriginal art. I retrieved my mobile telephone messages and responded. I bought a newspaper and caught up with Modesty Blaise.

Early in the afternoon Kaye and Rachel were taken to the airport and bid adieu. We all felt a sense of finality and loss. Then we picked up the motor cycle, checked oil levels and tyre pressures, checked the V4's chain tension and lubricated it and generally made sure that all was in readiness for the return journey. We were now two thirds of the way through the trip and this combined with the recent departure of wives and a mother lent a sombre air to the proceedings.

In our accommodation beside the lake we watched the West Coast Eagles demolish a hapless Hawthorn, despite kicking about 25 points, and slapped at mosquitoes. In the cool of the evening we had a drink and listened to the frogs. There were many forced jokes but no real hilarity. We dined quietly and talked about our trip next day to Wolf Creek Crater.

Lake Argyle is one of Australia's treasures. Please keep it that way for Tim Winton and me.

Chapter 39.
Day 16. 31 July.
Kununurra to Wolf Creek Crater and back to Halls Creek.

We packed early and left Kununurra by 7.30 a.m. I rode behind the Range Rover at a steady 110 to 120kmh for an uneventful run to Doon Doon. The scenery, as it so often does in the Kimberleys, made the ride an enjoyable experience. The hills are big and ancient. Some are rounded and seamed with crevasses formed by water erosion over the eons and some are crowned with layers of harder rock that have resisted wear. We paltry humans are such late arrivals on our planet that it is strange that we have come to the conclusions of our own importance that we have. Wedge tailed eagles soared overhead, the temperature was comfortable and all was right with the world. Because we were travelling west and south I had lost the diamonds that had glittered in the highway and on each side of it as I had travelled the other way but now I had company. My shadow, sometimes in front of me and sometimes to one side, faithfully nodded its head every time the V4 hit irregularities in the road. Although we had only covered 110 kilometres the boys stopped at Doon Doon. Hans could go no further without sustenance. We filled the vehicles' petrol tanks. The V4 had swallowed only 5 litres. After Doon Doon the scenery is a bit less interesting. The Kapok trees in full and glorious, buttercup yellow bloom that had lined the road gave way to termite mounds in a range of colours from dun grey to dark, dried blood reddish brown. Termite mounds are one of the icons of the north. The other is the Boab tree and both vary enormously. Some of the termite mounds are Gaudiesque in shape and others have the spare elegance of great gothic architecture. Others resemble nothing so much as a gigantic pile of elephant ordure. Some of the Boab trees are many stemmed as the Durack tree is and some have a large single bole as the "Gaol Tree" at Derby has. Some are relatively slender and tall and some are squat with short arms for branches. Impressive they might be but beautiful they are not.

As I wended my way to Halls Creek at legal speeds I found myself wondering what the greatest of humankind's inventions are. Not only what the greatest are but which are the least desirable? Even for a limited individual such as I am there are many to choose from. Are the Gods of one sort and another our greatest invention? We have invented many over the centuries from the pantheons of ancient Egypt, classical Greece and all conquering Rome to the many of India and points further east. Every group appears to have invented their own Gods. About 1300 years before Christ, when the fashion was for Pantheons of Gods, Akhenaton, then Pharaoh of Egypt, invented a single God – Amon. His God did not last long but the seed was sown and others took up the one true God theme. Now we have several one true Gods. Are they our greatest invention? They have certainly had a powerful influence on humankind. They have been responsible for many of our greatest buildings and many of our greatest endeavours. They have often led to us behaving in different ways – some noble and admirable and some despicable. There is a line of thought that without a deity we would misbehave more abominably than we do. Is this true? If we did not have the threat of eternal damnation and the carrot of eternal bliss hanging over us would we behave differently and worse? That is doubtful. History appears to show that followers of any one of the "one true Gods" behave at least as badly as "heathens". Ask those who were unlucky enough to have been in the World Trade Centre. Will we ever arrive at an answer to these difficult questions? I concluded that although deities are a wonderful product of the human mind and despite the great things that have been done in their names, they have been too destructive to be thought of as our greatest invention. Why they were invented and whether the human race would have been better off without them are questions I would like to see pursued. Many atrocities have been committed by many megalomaniacs in their names and many lives have been cut short by the lure of paradise for those prepared to die for their one true God.

Perhaps logic is our greatest invention. It certainly has adherents but if it is our greatest invention why is it abandoned so frequently? Is intuition the one? I have seen it defeat logic and it certainly has many adherents, especially on the distaff side.

Are the many mechanical inventions from the wheel to interstellar space craft the greatest things we have invented? Are these more important than the treatment and disposal of sewage? What about the blessed relief of pain killers from aspirin to the supreme knock out of general anaesthesia?

How about the cultivation of plants and animals for food? That invention led to *Homo sapiens* changing from being a hunter gatherer to settling in one place, which in turn led to civilisation and the building of our great cities. Perhaps the buildings that civilisations have produced are our greatest works. The Hagia Sophia? The Ise Shrine? Machu Picchu? The Parthenon and the Pantheon? Chartres Cathedral? Reims Cathedral? The Taj Mahal? The Kremlin? The Golden Gate Bridge? The Pyramids? or some of the many wonders produced during the reign of Rameses II – Abu Simbel, the temples at Thebes? There are many magnificent building works from which to choose including some later efforts such as the Sydney Opera House, Petronas Towers or the Guggenheim Museum in New York.

Are the vehicles, the trains, cars, buses, ships and aeroplanes that provide us with such freedom of movement our crowning achievement? Is our invention of the control of electrical power our greatest invention? It has certainly led to making life for those that have it available, a great deal more comfortable – but now its production is said by some to be poisoning our globe.

Is the computer our crowning achievement? What about the marvellous inventions that have enabled us to battle disease and now show promise of lengthening our lives even more substantially? How about the invention of interest on capital that allows so many unproductive members of society to live off the productive members and feel quite comfortable about it?

Humankind has invented many things that have helped our comfort and our productivity. Is this a good thing? Is that part of humanity who now wallow in luxury, who are demanding ever more freedom of movement and luxury and who are busily overeating happier than that part of humanity who are sweating and struggling? Each must make his or her own judgement.

And what are our worst inventions?

Is the invention and growth of tribalism that leads us into destroying each other and some of our better physical creations our worst invention? Is it the invention of Gods in whose name we have treated each other frighteningly badly at times and continue to do so? Are the explosives that create such havoc and which destroy so much, from gunpowder to the nuclear devices that have the potential to wipe life as we know it from our blue globe, our worst invention? Is power generation, on which we are hooked, and that could now be polluting our world, a benefit or a curse? Are our many wondrous vehicles, vehicles that provide us with such freedom of travel but that could also be polluting our world, our best invention? Or is our worst problem not an invention but just our nature?

Have we already produced our best and our worst?

Will our populations continue to grow in number, spread out to cover all available land and pollute our world like a brown virus until we have ruined the means of our livelihood – our Earth – as so many more limited civilisations have in the past? Take Easter Island as an example.

Or will we find the various forms of mental and physical energy necessary to carry our life form into space and colonise other worlds? Perhaps we will mutate into a better, more intelligent and altogether more admirable creature.

Perhaps we will continue with our silly squabbles over our Gods and our tribal boundaries until great numbers are destroyed so that the globe will then have to support far fewer – a task that it will then be able to do without being over taxed as it appears to be at present. May be – just may be – we will learn our lessons and start supporting each other, we will stop following leaders bent on their own personal power and we will answer the challenges of controlling our numbers and building better and fairer civilisations. I am not optimistic.

I would be delighted for my children, their children and their children's children if we could learn to live together and combine our efforts to meet the real challenges of existence and progress. The big challenges are not our tribal boundaries and our religious beliefs, as so many now appear to believe, but survival of our species and overcoming the destructive elements of human nature. Why, I asked myself, do so many of our kind strive for authority over others, strive to accumulate wealth and property that they cannot really use and try to impose their particular beliefs on those who would be happier without them? What is wrong with us and what can we do about such weaknesses?

Head abuzz with such thoughts I rode along sinking slowly into a greying mood. There was only one answer. Forgetting the added pollution I turned up the wick. If you ride a motorcycle quickly enough all else becomes secondary. I was encouraged into this course of action somewhat by two blokes on large single cylinder road/trail bikes who steamed past me. I theorised that if I arrived in Halls Creek well before the boys I could make all the arrangements for storing the bike and the trailer while we took off for Wolf Creek Crater before they arrived, and we looked as though we would be limited for time to do all we had to do. A slight right hand movement brought a satisfactory response from the VFR. It was running like a dream. I settled on a speed of between 140 and 160kph. The wind had blown up a bit so I was getting buffeted but that only made me concentrate more on business. I passed the pair on their road/trail bikes. They had stopped to take a short walk, probably to smell the flowers.

Hurtling along the Tanami Track at a furious pace.

Soon I trundled into Halls Creek. There I arranged to store the trailer with the Wheatleys who run the motel and parked and covered the bike. The team arrived; we parked the trailer safely, bought some take away, filled the Range and left for Wolf Creek Crater with Hans driving.

Hans likes driving quite quickly in difficult conditions on corrugated, loose gravel roads and did so. He must get his yearning for risk taking from his mother. I decided that my nervous system would be best served if I closed my eyes so I dozed. We saw the mound of the Crater from a long way off. It is the only feature on the scrubby plain and we arrived at it a good deal more quickly than we had estimated, no doubt due to the speed at which the ground had been covered. We parked near its base and approached it.

Nick and I climbed to the Crater's rim and started circling the dish. The independent Mr. H. Bruechle walked down into the Crater by himself. After we had covered about a quarter of the rim and had taken many photographs we returned to the starting place and met Hans who had just returned. He went back to the car and Nick and I descended into the Crater.

The Crater is just that. It is a great circular bath tub, about a kilometre across, which has been created by a meteorite. In the middle is a circle of low, scruffy growth that is probably supported by the rain that accumulates in the bath tub when it, infrequently, rains and it grows out of an area that is white due to salts that have been leached to the surface. The inner slopes of the circular hill that surrounds the crater are sparsely vegetated but there is a patch of sculptured white gums on the south east face and various small plants elsewhere. On the top of the rim there are small and delicately shaped shrubs.

Tne imprressive Wolf Creek Crater, formed many moons ago by a meteorite.

The walk, on what was a fairly warm day by then, was testing but not really difficult. Nick stayed with me most of the way but he could not resist a bit of a gallop up the rim and down the other side so he disappeared and I caught up with him and Hans back at the car park. They were discussing important issues of the day with a young couple from Victoria who, with their toddler, had just driven the Tanami Track in their 4 wheel drive and had not found it unduly difficult.

Nick drove back to Halls Creek where we washed underclothes, spent the late

Your correspondent on the crater rim.

Sunday afternoon watching football on TV and wondering how we had managed to fit so much into so short a period. After sundown the boys went to dinner. I was too tired to join them so I ate some fruit and made some notes before bedding. Tomorrow was to be another big day.

Chapter 40.
Day 17. 1 August.
Halls Creek to Broome.

Another early departure and we were away from Halls Creek. I have not written much about Halls Creek in this because there is not a lot to tell. There is a main street with a couple of service stations, the well run and hospitable motel at which we stayed, a hospital, a school, several shops, the shire offices and an impressive grassed oval on which has been deposited many beer containers.

If the town has a unique feature it is its liquor outlets. Outside each of these there are bollards to protect them from ram raids. Their windowless galvanized iron walls are heavy protection against illegal entry. They are pill boxes that provide protection for their contents which are, apparently, precious. I am not unduly sensitive to ambience but I felt a sense of pointlessness about the town – a lack of optimism and purpose – a sadness. This was reinforced for me by the singing I heard one night from the permanent camp at the edge of town. The songs were popular but the tone was melancholy to my, admittedly insensitive, ears. Maybe it was just my imagination on the night.

Halls Creek needs a purpose in life other than filling the tanks of traveller's cars and spending welfare cheques. We all need a purpose in life of course. Our early purposes were to survive – to obtain enough food to avoid starvation

– and to keep the species in existence. Now that the need to spend large portions of our energy in the pursuit of food has been fulfilled by agriculture and animal husbandry, other forms of purpose, other demands on our time and our energies, are necessary. I think that this applies to all living creatures on the earth but it applies especially to humankind.

When our basic needs are met art and culture can flower. We can create and build. We can explore. We can philosophise and work on abstruse mathematical theories. We can spend our intellectual effort in overcoming disease. We become fulfilled in other ways. There appear to be groups in our society who believe that all that has to be provided for happy humans to peacefully exist is sufficient food and comfort. They believe that spreading the wealth will create harmonious conditions and that the problems of the world are brought about by inequities in the "system". I do not so believe.

They consider that the problems of indigenous Australians have been brought about by the invasion of white settlers a couple of hundred years ago. If invasion by outsiders is the cause of the problems Europe, with its many invasions over the millennia, would not have reached the heights of productivity and cooperation it has. Let us hope old Europe successfully survives the current Muslim invasion it is undergoing and benefits from it as it has from invasions in the past.

If the aim is to make the lives of indigenous people happy surely what should be being searched for are challenges and purposes for them, not further hand outs. There are already useful directions being taken, of course, in the flowering of indigenous art and in those with the knowledge spreading indigenous mythology to an interested world, but other useful directions are necessary.

It has always seemed to me that people are at their best and most contented when they are serving their society in some way. This is not a belief that is widely held today, when happiness is generally equated with having possessions in the greater part of the world, but I believe that belief is only a passing, and not very successful, phase. Contentment lies in contribution, not in accumulation. Happiness lies in doing useful or interesting things, not in receiving hand outs or in changing perception with drugs. Satisfaction comes from understanding, meaning that education is its key. But how do you educate those who do not want to be educated?

We travelled west out of the town. Because that was the direction of our travel I still had my shadow for company mimicking my every move. There was a good deal of fresh road kill and eagles irritatedly took off as I approached. The V4 was purring like a happy tiger and I was relaxed at between 110 and 120kph. As we filled the tanks and left town the temperature was 16 C but it warmed as the day advanced and we moved further west.

Fitzroy Crossing arrived in good time and I stopped for breakfast knowing that Hans, at least, would not be able to go much further without calories. We filled the tanks and left on what was to be my longest single stint in the saddle up until then. I did not need to refuel at Willare and I still had plenty up my sleeve when I got to the Roebuck turn off so I carried on to Broome – over 400k. It was quite a long period in the saddle but I was road hardened by that time and it was made relatively easy by the route being through great country on a good road in warm conditions.

Because I was trapped inside my helmet and the road was not taxing, my mind turned back to some of its meanderings of yesterday. I asked myself why the many who believe in a specific God, even though they must know that humankind has been inventing Gods of various descriptions since before the dawn of civilisation when there were only small, nomadic tribes, deny that any God other than their own has any validity?

Many in the past, especially those that believed in the more recent monotheistic religions, were often prepared to become aggressively angry and do most ungodlike things to those who disagreed with them. No monotheistic religion has a clean slate of course but only the Muslim religion, the newest of the monotheistic religions, now has many adherents who encourage punitive action against those who do not hold with their particular God.

Why were Gods invented at all? All other forms of animal life appear to struggle through their tenures on the globe without Gods to support them. When I stand on a snail I doubt that its last thought as my foot descends is "This is God's punishment?"

Are Gods necessary to control the behaviour of groups? Can't we behave reasonably without a higher being that will reward or punish us? Is it because life is so unenjoyable that we have to believe in a hereafter to make our present existence bearable? May be we lesser beings enjoy the pomp and ceremony associated with religions and their edifices and need something to look up to and aspire to.

I defy anyone to go to the Vatican or one of the other great places of worship such as Cologne Cathedral, the Sagrada Familia, the Blue Mosque or the Ise Shrine and not be impressed. But then I defy anyone to look at the works of the Pharaohs, the living Gods of Egypt, or the temples of ancient Greece and not be similarly impressed.

It was the invention of the several One True Gods that led to many of the most iniquitous actions of human history. Each of the groups who invented, found or discovered their One True God often then assumed that their God was not only the best and only God but that it was their duty to cram their God down the throat of others. It still goes on with Muslims stating quite clearly that there will never be peace until all humankind submits to the one true religion – Islam.

When will we humans move away from such pitiful concepts? Are we able to? Will the world be a better place if we do? There is now so much capital and emotional investment in the God industry that God is unlikely to die out in the near future. It is a worry that at least one God is having a resurgence and that many of that God's followers are quite prepared to slaughter non-believers. Will knowledge and education finally prevail and the current crop of monotheistic Gods fade into being an interesting phenomenon of the past as the living Gods that were the Pharaohs or the Gods who lived on Olympus or in Valhalla have? Or will one God conquer all?

Would the earth be a better place if we humans stopped believing that each of us is so important that we all merit a personal God who takes a personal interest in each of us – that we realised each of us is unimportant in the great scheme of the universe? If we did reach that conclusion would each of us then behave better, or worse?

I was on my own on a reliable machine on a good road in country that was becoming less interesting as I travelled west at an unexciting legal speed. Solitude brought more pondering. This time about the isms that have been so important during my life span. The two that have driven our main societies forward recently are capitalism and communism, although fascism had an important turn at the wheel when I was a boy.

Which, as I have asked myself many times in the past, is better – communism with its call for "from each according to his ability and to each according to his needs" or capitalism with its drive for wealth accumulation, never mind the ultimate cost?

On the surface communism wins by several lengths in a canter. There have been many fine human beings who have subscribed to the creed and have tried to live to its requirements. Yet capitalism has been successful. Why? The problem seems to be that in communist states those greedy for power float to the top. Look at Lenin, Stalin and Mao. In capitalist societies those greedy for wealth float to the top.

Neither might be desirable but history has clearly shown that those greedy for wealth are far less likely to do short term damage than those greedy for power, and the short term is all most of us seem to care about. Would the world not be a better and easier place in which to live if the leaders were not driven by either personal power or pelf? Would a better world not be possible in the longer term if we all, including our leaders, woke up to the fact that succeeding in our own spheres but damaging the whole damages us all quite personally?

This led me on to considering why we in the western world, through our honours systems and our various press outlets, are so admiring of those greedy people who accumulate great wealth through the efforts of others, especially if they hand back a proportion of what they have taken in some philanthropic way.

The financial press daily deifies these greedy people whose main aim has been to accumulate wealth, even if they have not been too scrupulous about how they have done that. The press reports on the accumulation in glowing terms. The facts that vast wealth can only be gained by blind luck, great innovative skill or by giving less to those that have actually produced something than they have earned and keeping the difference, seems to have evaded the press.

When a smugly smiling billionaire donates a painting to an art gallery or endows a hospital to fund a ward because one of the billionaire's children has a disease or a genetic defect the press duly reports on their generosity. Honours are then bestowed by a grateful state. Why is it that importance to society is so often equated to the accumulation of wealth in our western societies? Perhaps it is. Does my dislike of the present system spring purely from jealousy or am I right in believing that those who quietly contribute are more worthy of the state's accolades than those already bathed in luxury or able to strike a cricket ball with authority? Is a person who has devoted a life to quietly serving others not more worthy of an honour than someone who accumulates wealth from their society and then gives some of it back – tax exempt? May be we will learn something from the scandal breaking in the UK about the buying of honours as I write this, but, based on past performances it is unlikely. What is likely is that the scandal will just fade away as journalists demonstrate their notoriously short attention spans.

Having decided that there was nothing terribly admirable in the accumulation of great wealth I then concentrated on the reasons people do it. Why do they drive themselves so wholeheartedly to making money? No one enjoys being poor and hungry but after a comfortable level is achieved why accumulate more, and more, and more?

Some, I suppose, get caught up in a gigantic game of Monopoly. Some probably just suffer from the unpleasant character trait of greediness. Some probably get started and find it difficult to stop. I think though that most are driven by inner insecurities. They need to succeed in the area of wealth accumulation because they are unsure of themselves and their worth and they need a marker to prove to themselves they are worthwhile – the marker of wealth and public accolade. They gain their feeling of self worth because our society does not condemn those who manipulate others for their own personal gain. On the contrary – they congratulate and honour them.

I know that an argument can be made that without people driving forward our society would not develop, but people with courage, energy, imagination and ability do change the world without accumulating much of its wealth. It is my opinion that no CEO or Chairperson of any company should be paid at an hourly rate more than 20 times the rate of the least paid person on the staff. Now that would change the world – and in my opinion for the better. I rode into Broome with these thoughts bouncing around in my head.

Nick had arranged accommodation for us there. The only accommodation he could find, or said he could find, was the Mercure, and only then because I am a member of Accor. It was luxury, but at a price. The Mercure is on the site of the old Continental Hotel.

The "Conti" was a galvanized iron, airy, open to the outside drinking hole with a "Broome" atmosphere and ambience. It was once the centre of the town's social life. Ken, Cyril and I had a memorable first night in Broome there many years ago playing darts, meeting the locals and getting a feel for what was the most cosmopolitan place I had ever been in, and that included London's Soho.

At that time Ken was the President of the Royal Perth Golf Club and he was widely known so I was not surprised when a well dressed man with an upper crust English accent said "Well, hallo Ken. What are you doing here? Staying with Guy?" Ken said no. He then asked if Ken was staying at the Continental. Ken again said no. So he asked "Well where are you staying?" Cyril, the ever helpful Cyril, decided to take a hand. He said "We are staying at the Cable Hilton". This caused Michael, for that was his name, to go into paroxysms of guffaws between which he spluttered "The President of Royal Perth Golf Club is sleeping on Cable beach. How precious. I'll be able to dine out on this for months". I came to the conclusion that he was a first class pillock. However after he had had a couple of beers he thawed and invited us to join him in what was then the town blood house, the Roebuck. Guided by a Michael who was by that time well lubricated we braved the "Roey", where we found that not only did we fit in quite nicely but that everyone in the bar seemed to know Michael. He had transformed from English git to the bar flies' mate in the space of only a couple of hours. Even his accent changed. We did not hear any more about him dining out on Ken's accommodation. After the bar shut we wended our way across the plain to Cable beach where Cyril slaughtered his deflating air mattress with an entrenching tool, and from then on slept on the front seat of the Land Rover and Ken and I bedded down in the moonlight in our sleeping bags on our air mattresses under a many starred limpid sky. Peace, perfect peace.

The unique and quite wonderful "Conti" has gone for good and has been replaced by a very nice, clean, well run and excellently catered hotel, but it has the same ambience as any other hotel from San Francisco to Qatar. Something has been lost never to be regained. The wonderful, galvanised iron Conti' and its range of local characters is no more. There is no doubt that we tourists, searching as we do for different worlds, destroy what we are looking for just by going there. Hans and I shared a room and Nick was, purportedly, on his own. But who is to know?

Late in the afternoon Hans took off with his mate Greg and Nick and I wandered out to Cable Beach and sat on a veranda with a couple of beers to watch the sun go down over the ocean. The spectacle was not helped by the other 5000 people similarly engaged and fighting for tables but the light there still has a special quality that reminded me of late afternoon in the Greek Cyclades and we enjoyed it.

Once the sun had disappeared we wended our way back to the Mercure and played pool – or rather Nick played pool, I merely knocked balls into positions where Nick could sink them easily – and drank more beer. We had a good dinner and managed to drink more beer while we settled some of the world's problems.

It is a vast pity that those that understand the world's problems are too busy drinking beer or driving taxis to actually get out there and fix things so the operation of the world is left to politicians who, as everybody knows, do not have a clue.

It had been a long day and it had had its regrets. We had bypassed both Windjana and Geikie Gorges in our headlong rush. I would like to have revisited them but our program was too tight to fit them in. Next time! After Nick and I retired to read Hans, the playboy of the Kimberleys, turned up in a pain-free state and we bedded.

"The V4 was purring like a happy tiger and I was relaxed at between 110 and 120kph."

Chapter 39.
Day 18. 2 August.
Broome to Cape Keraudren.

We left the luxury of the Mercure with some regret and headed down the road. We were unlikely to have salubrious surroundings again on this trip. The first 33k to Roebuck is east and north, and then we started the long trek south.

This section of the journey, down through Sandfire to Pardoo is not exciting scenery so my mind, which by now you should have realised has a mind of its own, wandered to some of the imponderables of long distance motorcycling. Why is it that 50km first thing in the morning is so easy to accomplish and is so quickly covered when 50km late in the afternoon takes so appallingly long when you are hot and sweaty or, worse, cold and stiff.

Then, after I had passed a couple of caravans, my mind moved on to considering the morals, ethics, economics and long term effects of us humans using up the sun's stored energy to tow our homes behind us across the plains of northern Australia. How long will we be able to do so? Should we be doing so? There is no doubt that my generation has been a privileged group. We have been able to travel the world, to eat well (many have gourmandised to excess), to communicate with others in all parts of our globe and to learn of mysteries and matters unheard of only 100 years ago. We have seen the commencement of space travel and we have seen several of us land on the moon.

We have been enabled to do these things by burning the oil, gas and coal stored many millions of years ago as great forests and colonies of animal life became buried. Our civilisations are now completely dependent on this ancient largesse of the sun. How long will we be able to use these finite resources? What effect will our profligate use of them have on our globe? For how long will we be able to maintain these privileges? Are the doomsayers who predict massive solar warming right or are those who say that the small amount of carbon dioxide that is being added to an atmosphere made up almost totally of nitrogen and oxygen will have little effect and that the global warming that is being experienced is due to much more deep seated changes than humankind's petty meddling?

Is water vapour a greater producer of "the greenhouse effect" than CO2? Can we humans control the amount of water vapour the sun takes from our oceans? Will any action taken by Australia, which produces well under 2% of the world's CO2, change anything anyway? We perhaps should show leadership but will any difference be made by whatever we do? So many questions. So few clear answers. We must consider these questions further – but in a balanced manner. Could it be that too many leading lights in this complex field are making a handsome and self-important living out of their pronouncements?

No wonder human societies flock to any Messiah who says they have an answer, no matter how misguided it might be. Anyone who can convince themselves of something has no trouble getting a following. The Germanic tribes are superior and deserve to inherit the earth! Certainly Adolph! We will follow you. There is only one true God. His name is Allah and all others should be subservient to true believers! Too right Osama! Let's show the world that our God will brook no resistance. Death to infidels! Christianity is the greatest religion and Christians should control the world! Absolutely! Let's all rush off to a new Crusade and convert the "savages" of the world to our way of thinking. Democracy is the only sound political system despite its many flaws! Right again George Bush. Saddam Hussein cannot be allowed to continue to get away with what he has been doing even if Robert Mugabe can. As you can see from these few examples – it is difficult to please everybody.

Will cutting down on the use of fossil fuel change the world for the better and prevent climate change – even though there have been massive changes in the past, long before humankind existed? Yes, of course it will. That nice Al Gore said so.

In any event, given our dependence on the sun's energy what can we do about the present power production systems? Are the sources touted as "renewable energy" really renewable or will their use have unintended side effects? Is wind power really a viable option given the energy that has to be expended to make and service the huge towers? Is tidal power or wave power viable? Is direct use of the sun's rays through solar cells the answer? Will great reflecting mirrors that focus the sun's energy to a point solve our problems? Have those who are advocating these approaches thought their way through the whole equation? I doubt it.

Although those advocating "clean energy" often quote the high costs, and say we must afford them regardless of the cost, I have yet to see any energy in/energy out equations on any of the avenues being pursued. For instance, if wind towers do not produce a good deal more power than that which goes into manufacturing, constructing and maintaining them they are not worthwhile, given that they are not constant power sources and that they have noise and other ecological shortcomings, but no one I know of has produced any research on the balance as I write this in 2006. If there is such basic research why has it not been widely circulated? Is the extra energy involved in making double glazing recouped, with interest, in the energy savings double glazing provides in the lifetime of the building double glazed? If not it should not be considered.

Why have those involved in these wondrous technological developments not started with energy saving equations? I suspect it is because such equations do not justify the use of these "Green Energy" experiments and the technologist's fun would be spoiled. The green energy advocates appear to be either those who have not considered the real issues but want to believe they are saving the world from itself or they have an interest in the funding being provided for the research. Green energy is an issue for which emotion has outrun logic. We need more basic thinking involved.

When the sun's precious energy, stored in coal, oil and gas deposits runs out will that stop our wanderings or will we come up with new ways to exploit the sun's benevolence, such as efficiently harnessing tidal power, heat from the depths of our globe and wind power and if we do harness them what long term effects might that have?

What is the future of Plutonium or Thorium power? Are those methods of producing our much needed electrical power really so dangerous or are these, again, an emotional issue? Is the residue really toxic and of no value?

This led on to the consideration of what the real problem probably is. I came to the unhappy conclusion that there are probably too many human beings in the world. If there are too may people and if their activities are polluting our globe then is there any humane solution? As David Suzuki has pointed out the human population has trebled – note – trebled – since he was born, and he is considerably younger than I am. This overcrowding can lead to more or less tolerance. I hope that it leads to more but I fear that it will lead to less.

Will the overcrowding and the sensibilities of the religious fundamentalists lead to holocaust? Is self destruction humankind's fate? Or will we slowly poison the Earth until we can no longer exist on it in our present numbers? This is what apparently happened to the Easter Islanders and to the Maya.

This is all profoundly depressing but these are the questions to which we should be turning our best brains. Instead we argue about our borders, our forms of government, which resources we can exploit and, perhaps worst and most destructively of all, our Gods.

Are there any answers? Will research and education rid us of our stupidities and our destructive beliefs? Will people learn that satisfying their immediate needs, greeds and self importances is not in our world's best interests and therefore not in their best personal interests? Will we find a way out of what appears to be a whole of life threatening mess?

The road wound on. Despite sitting in one position at an unexciting speed these thoughts and a certain amount of singing into my helmet kept me awake enough to respond to the occasional bends.

My mind would not lie down and happily doze as I asked it to. Instead I asked myself the less demanding question as to whether the manner in which my Australian society is treating its indigenous citizens is reasonable. I concluded that I do not think so but I failed to come up with solutions as to what should be done – only more questions – and there are too many of those already.

The children so often start out as smiling, clear skinned, bright eyed youngsters and die at a young age after an unhappy and sordid existence. It seems obvious that the way in which many are living is sad and without hope.

Is the answer to be that the rest of the society who lives in this land should give them more of what we have gained from the country we all live in or must they make their own way in a society that is, perhaps, alien to their nature? Does providing them with material things and freedom of access to alcohol help them or will these provisions by the immigrant part of our society, on the face of it only reasonable, slowly destroy a culture and a people?

Isn't any human better off if they contribute to their society as best they can? Should the rest of us try to get them to join us in one unified society or should they carry on with their own unique ways? Should any Australian be treated differently to any other because of their skin colour or because they, or their parents, or grandparents or great, great, great grandparents were born somewhere else on our tiny globe?

Surely equality of opportunity is all any citizen should be able to ask of his or her society. No one should expect equality of outcome because each of us has different abilities. Obviously it is in our society's best interests to make the lot of all, including those with an indigenous background, as good and as pleasant and productive as it can be but how is this best accomplished?

I would dearly have loved to have played cricket for Australia but I was never selected. Is this because I was discriminated against or is it because I have limited ball sense?

Difficult stuff and I doubt that there is an "answer" but we must try because we now have many sad and frustrated citizens rotting away. Should we agree with those who claim that as the country was stolen from their ancestors 200 years ago those who have descended from the original inhabitants are entitled to continuing largesse or should we believe Noel Pearson, who says that his people must learn to help themselves in the world in which they now live?

If the first of these alternatives is the correct one can the Celts, Picts and Scots claim they should be supported by the Angles, Saxons, Jutes, Vikings, Romans and Normans who invaded their lands? History would need to be re-written.

If Noel Pearson is correct how can those of aboriginal descent become part of contemporary society except through education? And will those being educated find the education that is being provided interests them, is regarded by them as being relevant and attracts them, or will they be bored and skip classes?

These are serious and difficult questions. Are these and other questions that vitally affect our society best left in the hands of politicians with their desire to be re-elected and, stemming from that, their four year focus, which can cause them to think of popular, short term, tactical answers to questions, not strategic long term solutions? Is our democracy working? Is a better system possible? No decisions, only questions that need answers. We must continue to consider and find balanced answers to these questions.

A decision I did make was that I would like to fill up both the Range Rover and the V4 at Pardoo, not earlier. The reason for this was that I wanted to curry favour with the service station proprietor so that I could leave the bike safely there overnight while we went out and camped at Cape Keraudren.

Nick pulled into Sandfire but I waved him on. The flaw in my logic was that the V4 was chewing up juice a good deal faster than it had the day before and it appeared more than likely that I would run out short of Pardoo. I contented myself with the thought that there were jerry cans full of premium fuel on the trailer. The bike eventually tossed in the towel at 458km, just 8km from our destination. That is not bad for a 21 litre tank. When we did get there we filled up – the Range was also down to the dregs – we ate a service station sandwich each and I parked the VFR in a fenced section of the service station yard under its plastic cover. Then we set forth for the Cape.

Cape Keraudren has a special place in my memory and in my heart. I first went there with Cyril and Ken on our odyssey from Broome to Perth via points of interest in the early 1970's. When we bumped down the wheel rutted track in the late afternoon there was a vast pond of water surrounded by beaches, incredibly sharp rocks on which small but tasty oysters were packed and small forests of mangroves. Six hours later there were just pools, channels and rills in the rippled silty sand of the bay. It was a beautiful place. There were turtles, flying fish that sparkled as they leapt, sinister swirls in the deeper water created by some marine monsters, birds flying and diving over those swirls and giant clams, warm red cliffs and magnificent light. The place, which we then had to ourselves, was like no other I had ever seen. In the pools there were octopuses that obligingly squirted water and ink at us when we disturbed them and at night the hermit crabs came out to maraud.

At the time I thought that it was a wonderland that someone should exploit and I dreamed of creating a development that would attract people from all over the world. I have since changed my mind and now want it reserved for only me and any of my friends that I think should be given the privilege of a visit.

Now, unfortunately for conservationists such as Tim Winton and me, others have found out about it and they have detracted from the glory I once knew. Such special places should be reserved for only sensitive souls, with either Tim or me deciding who is sensitive enough to be granted the privilege of a visit.

These photos show the bay at Cape Keraudren near low tide at sunset and near high tide during the day.

As I told you earlier I once spent an evening there in the rain with Paul Bennett teasing the octopuses by torchlight and again we had it to ourselves. Unfortunately in my enthusiasm to show some of its wonders to Paul I lost the car and only found it as the torch gave out. I also went there with Bob Allan and we, again, were the only people there and on the eighty mile beach. Now the beach is a speedway for four wheel drive vehicles. As I reported in Chapter 10 I attempted to take Nick out to the Cape previously on the BMW motor cycle trip but we were defeated by deep sand and washaways. When Hans was about 5 years old Kaye, Nick, he and I camped there on our journey to Queensland across the bottom of the Gulf of Carpentaria. By that time it was already becoming popular.

Now Keraudren has many, many caravans and trailer homes all with their own little generators thudding away and satellite dishes so that their owners can watch "Home and Away" and enjoy all the comforts of suburbia, which they could have enjoyed in suburbia. They have, of course, the pioneering discomfort of strange smelling toilets perched at the ends of ramps, which are a hardship to the sensitive, but it is no longer necessary to squat over holes dug with an entrenching tool. I liked it better before – or is my happy memory clouded by age and sifted through time?

We unpacked, what in comparison to some of those around us was our primitive camp, and then wandered out into a bay that was drying as the tide fell. I have to report that the bay still drains to rippled silty flats, the octopuses still squirt, the flying fish still fly and dark shapes still swim rapidly below the surface. The light remains special and the whole place retains its unique air. It is a magnificent place and it must be looked after. During our walk a pelican came and molested us, no doubt looking for food. After we had terrorized the octopuses and photographed the water snails we went ashore, dried our feet and drove over to the south end of the Eighty Mile Beach.

The big sky and blissful solitude of the 80 Mile Beach at Cape Keraudren.

We set up the Keraudren Camp towards sunset.

The rippled silt flats of the bay at Cape Keraudren at low tide. The patterns and muted colours are exquisite.

One of the creatures who come out to feed at low tide. When examined closely the area is a wonderland.

There are many octopuses lying in shallow pools at low tide. They are beautiful, fluidly moving creatures.

Out on the flats Hans and Nick discovered a beady eyed friend who was very disappointed when no fish were forthcoming.

With the tide out the water is a long way from shore and the walk out on the flats is a rewarding experience as I had found previously with Ken and Cyril and later on my own and with Bob Allan. There are shells and skeletons of marine creatures of wondrous shapes and varieties in the grey silt. We did not have the opportunity for the walk this trip however. Hans cut his foot badly enough for us to return to camp in order to clean it up and to patch it. Nick and I had to do the surgery and that required steeling of the nerves and steadying of the hands, so we had a beer. Hans insisted on one also, as anaesthetic, and although Nick and I considered it a waste we gave him one. As the sun set in an amazing orange-golden glow we prepared a meal over our little gas fired, three burner camp stove (I did not say that we were completely primitive) and drank ice cold beer out of our, as time proved, inadequately stocked ice box to help overcome the trauma we were all feeling about the disaster of Hans's foot. After the meal and several more nerve settling beers we played cards in what I can only describe as a most unseemly and over competitive fashion. We bedded reasonably early because it was getting cold and because the beer ran out. It proved to be a chilly night and the sleeping bags were useful.

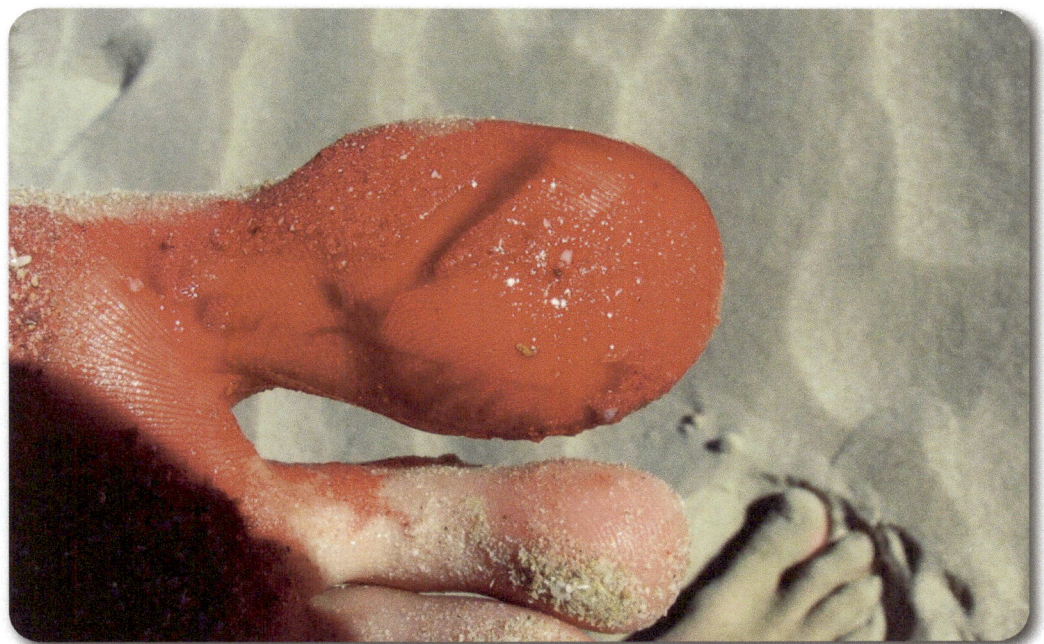
The gap in Hans's toe was bad enough to stop him walking but not bad enough for us to rush off to the nearest doctor.

Sunset over the bay at Cape Keraudren is a sight to behold.

Chapter 40.
Day 19. 3 August.
Cape Keraudren to Wickham.

We arose, a little cool and stiff, at day break. Hans was immobilised but Nick and I were keen to have a walk around the area before we left. It was a glorious morning. Out on the point where Paul and I had become bushed there was a young bloke fishing from the cliffs. He was lean, tanned and wirily muscled in his shorts, and he had a mop of long woolly hair. He was travelling alone but for the company of a guitar and was financing the trip by entertaining at pubs when he hit towns. His hopes of hooking into something major were boosted by schools of small fish shooting past the base of the cliffs pursued by ominous dark shapes. We amalgamated our optimism with his but nothing happened while we watched. However standing there on the cliff's edge with the sun warming us and with nature at its best spread out at our feet life was certainly worthwhile even if we were not to have the pleasure of watching a large fish being murdered. After a most enjoyable couple of hours of sauntering in ideal conditions Nick and I returned to Hans and the camp to pack.

Breaking camp and packing a trailer is always a new procedure. Nothing ever goes back exactly where it came from. This morning the difficulties of packing the trailer were compounded by the discovery that one of our water vessels had leaked, and wet a good deal of our gear. Eventually all was accomplished and we left with regret and drove over to Pardoo where we picked up the VFR.

We then headed for Port Hedland. Nobody wanted to stop there so on to the Whim Creek hotel we went. Whim Creek was once a place apart. Isolation breeds uniqueness and Whim Creek was once isolated. Only professional truckers, miners and odd hardy souls used to go there so it was a place where people were different.

I could tell tales about Ken winning pockets full of two shilling pieces playing hoop la and how he did it, or Cyril demonstrating how to achieve an alcoholic high for nothing by winning free beers at

The solitary fisherman on the point. Skipping bait fish and dark shapes following them kept him interested but fisherman's luck eluded him.

darts, or even the stir two young ladies created by fronting up in the noisy and disorganized bar in short shorts but that was in a different and scruffier Whim Creek. That was a Whim Creek with character where the truckies stood around fires after the pub' shut to sober up before they continued on their runs north and south and where we bedraggled tourists in our Land Rover went to sleep on the disused tennis court and awoke next morning feeling the worse for wear and had nowhere to shower. The Whim Creek of today has been modernized, sanitized and generally made to look like any other convenience stop. On this visit we noticed that the proprietors were extending it and modernizing it further, which will mean it will be even more homogenized. Now there is no camel to pester you for a beer. Once he asked for cans of beer and if you gave him one with the tag peeled off he would pick it up in his mouth, tilt his head back and drink it in one motion. He has been replaced by Barra Burgers but the exchange has been largely downhill. After we had demolished our Barra Burgers, which were quite edible, we hit the road. Our next stop was to be Roebourne.

Now Roebourne has undoubtedly been a wonderful place in its time but the accommodation there looked less than inviting and we wanted somewhere to wash our laundry so we moved on to Wickham where we found excellent, clean and comfortable accommodation at Wickham Lodge. Wickham is a place with all the wonders of our modern world – wonders that we all take for granted. For instance it has a comprehensive shopping mall where it is possible to buy all essentials from bait to beer and even such esoteric and frivolous items as fresh vegetables, butter and Kellogg's Corn Flakes. I do not want to make Wickham sound too attractive but it had one other feature of our modern world that I would be remiss not to report. It had – drum roll please – a booze bus, which we successfully avoided.

After settling in we drove out to Cossack, which now has people living there and has been "restored" so that it has lost the eerie spirit that pervaded it on earlier visits when it was deserted and tumbledown. Cyril, Ken and I once stood on the old jetty eating sandwiches in silence and each privately wondered what the place had been like when it was a bustling port. There is something ineffably sad about a once thriving human habitation that has failed and only the skeleton remains. There is something less than satisfying about a restored habitation with cars parked out the front of clean buildings. The boys were unimpressed. We drove further to a lookout where we admired, and photographed tidal flats gleaming in the afternoon light.

After wandering around for a while we returned to the Lodge, showered and went out to Point Sampson, another cleaned up place that has both gained and lost from its modernization, for an excellent meal with a good red while we sat on a balcony and enjoyed our holiday spirit. I told the boys the wonderful tale of Cyril White's catch after a day of fishing from the Point Sampson jetty. Have you ever heard of "Lizard" fish? Cyril has. He has caught them. Ken landed a shark.

The tidal flats near the point at Cossack glow in the afternoon sun.

Chapter 41.
Day 20. 4 August.
Wickham to Carnarvon.

We arose in leisurely fashion at Wickham, slowed down somewhat by the large meal of the night before, even though we had washed it down with a good deal of beer and red wine to lubricate its passage. At 8.30 we left and filled the tanks at Roebourne. The ride from Roebourne south is truly GAFA country.

GAFA is the description of uninteresting country that a photographer for the "West Australian" newspaper, Toj Campbell, was reported to have given to Viscount de Lisle, who was then the Governor of Western Australia, as they flew over a stretch of nothing much. Toj told the Governor that what was below them was great "GAFA" country. Ever the English aristocrat the Viscount asked Toj what that meant and Toj told him. "It stands for Great Australian F--k All your Lordship".

The ride took me south through scrubby flats with occasional reddish sand dunes running east and west through which the road had been cut and not much else until we reached the banana plantations near the Gascoyne River – a short distance from Carnarvon.

My mind was not under much pressure and it wandered into a consideration of the machine under me. At 5000rpm in sixth gear the bike covers approximately 2km per minute. This means that every kilometre requires the motor to go through at least 2500 cycles. Given that there is lower gear work and that I covered about 8000km it means that the motor went around at least 20 million times on the trip. We all take for granted such incredible reliability. It is a miracle of design, experience and construction expertise.

We bowled into Carnarvon in tandem and headed for an hotel/motel near the estuary we had stayed at previously. We booked into the "family suite" and unloaded. The quality of the accommodation had not improved since we had last stayed there and I will not be going back unless something changes. There was not even a mirror in either bathroom. Hans was not unduly upset by what was not there because there were two, count them – two, television sets.

Later, guided by Nick who has a great instinct for these things, we took a short cut from our digs to the "Old Post Office" restaurant that just about circumnavigated the town. There we partook of three of the "World's Best Pizzas", and they were bloody good. The walk back, which was not a short cut, took us less than half the time Nick's short cut had taken and we went early to bed where I read another chapter of "A Short History of Nearly Everything". It was not our most exciting day and the fact that we were heading home and that the adventure was nearing its end cast a slight mist of melancholy over the proceedings.

Riding through 'GAFA' country.

Chapter 42.
Day 21. 5 August.
Carnarvon to Dongara.

The scenery south of Carnarvon is not a vast improvement on that which had been served to us on the previous afternoon but I was enjoying it even less because the temperature had dropped to below 16 degrees. I should let non motorcyclists know a bit about motor cycle travel in cold weather. When the air temperature is below 20C body temperature drops due to the wind chill factor. In good gear the effect is minimized but after an hour or so riding can be fairly hard going and when the temperature is below 10C or rain is falling even a good jacket and gloves will not stop you stiffening up after about three quarters of an hour. Once you are cold it is a matter of grim determination and putting your hands down onto the motor to warm them when you can as you tear along trying to keep your concentration at a reasonable level.

    I have mentioned before in this that the thermometer on my V4 that tells me the ambient temperature or the temperature of the motor at the touch of a button. I am not sure of the value of this but I suppose it is nice to know that when you think your hands are freezing, your bum is numb and you feel as though you might never be able to straighten out again you are not imagining it. The same goes when you are sweating inside your jacket even though its vents are open to allow the wind in and the wind feels hot on your face. It is then very handy to know that the temperature is 42°C.

Another facet of long distance biking that might not have been appreciated by non-bikers is that you can get tired of sitting in the same position and that your wrists and shoulders can start to ache, especially if you are riding in buffeting winds or at high speed. These various aches, compounded in my case by advancing (some say advanced) age can be alleviated somewhat by changing your riding position or standing up on the foot pegs, doing deep knee bends and flexing calf muscles. I sometimes lie down with my chest on the tank bag and my feet anchored onto the pillion footrests. The only thing you cannot change, except for very brief periods, is the position of your right hand. That must remain on the twist throttle which keeps it within easy reach of the main stopper – the front wheel brake. I guess that non motorcyclists dream about the freedom of the open road and the thrill of speed but travel at 120kmh is not exciting. It is tedious and it can be soporific. The only way to relieve the tedium is to go fast and that is – alas – illegal so motorcyclists, who are by nature a law abiding lot as you have found from this story of our trip, do not speed except in emergencies and so they can suffer from boredom. Oh well – back to the road south of Carnarvon.

An hour or so on the road saw the temperature rise and wonderful carpets started to appear on each side of the bitumen. Fields of clean, white everlastings, acres of pale yellow puff balls of flowers, streams of royal purple pea shaped flowers on delicate stems, pink daisies, more white daisies and occasional stand alone plants with large, fleshy, bright pink flowers came into view and were passed. .Here and there were backdrops of wattles just coming into bloom. Nick and I were enchanted and stopped often to take photographs. Hans, who is much more mature than Nick and I and having seen so much of the world he was, at nineteen, weary of it all. He could not see what the fuss was about. Eventually, when the cards on my digital camera were full, I galloped off on my steed and left Nick to take close ups on his own.

I pulled up outside the "Miner's Arms" in Northampton and purchased three Emu Bitter stubbies from a charming and charmingly pneumatic young lady, with a bubbly personality who told me she was from Holland and had only been in Australia the standard three weeks. I sat outside in the sunshine and talked to a couple of other blokes who were filling in time until my thirsty sons arrived. When they had taken in Miss Holland and had read a sign that said tonight was skimpy night neither of them wanted to go further. However I told them that I had already checked out whether she was the entertainment

The glorious wildflowers of the Pilbara after rain. They are quite superb.

and she had said she was not so they agreed to go on. I still wonder whether or not she was.

After our stubbies had evaporated we continued. No matter how often I cover the distance from Northampton to Dongara I never tire of the Chapman Valley and the Greenough flats and I always remember the first time I saw them over sixty years ago when my father took my sister and I to Shark Bay one Christmas in his 1938 Ford V8. That was a difficult trip in another age. I skirted the fair town of Geraldton by taking the by pass road on which I was fortunate enough to arrive just as each of the traffic lights, of which there are many, were turning amber. I was pleased to see that although I had been away from traffic lights for a period I had not lost my touch with them and that I still had the ability to change them against me as I neared. As I waited at each light for the maximum period I realized that this gave me the time to be able to enjoy the fumes of the heavy traffic and to admire the colourful ambience and glow of the fast food outlets that seemed to be on most corners.

With Geraldton at last behind me I entered onto the Greenough flats in bright sunshine and dropping temperature. There is always a temptation to travel at greater than the speed limit on these straight roads with only one set of bends, and those bends can be taken at speed. Mr. Plod is also aware of this and tends to spoil the fun with his radar detectors and his Multanovas. There I was tooling along at just greater than the speed limit and starting to chill when a person in a hurry went past in his sedan. I tucked in behind knowing that if anyone was about to be fined for speeding it was unlikely to be me. I pulled in to the Dongara Hotel and booked rooms for all of us. As I walked out with keys the boys arrived so we parked and locked the trailer and took our gear into our rooms. We cleaned up and wandered over to the front bar where we played pool as the sun went down.

Previously, when Nick, Mike Bernoulli, a Singapore Airlines pilot, and I were in town riding down from Exmouth we ate at a restaurant named Takos and it was sensational so we went there again. It had changed hands and although it was still good it was no longer sensational. After the great expectations that had been aroused in Hans by stories of our previous visit by Nick and I, we all felt a little let down. May be it was that the food was not as good as expected and may be our let down was because it was our last night on the road and we were regretting that it was nearly over. After our meal and good red wine we ambled back to our rooms for a subdued last night.

More beautiful wildflowers.

Chapter 43.
Day 22. 6 August.
Dongara to Perth.

The road from Dongara to Perth is not the most scenic of the roads of WA but the road itself is good and it has its winding sections that keep up rider interest. This was it. It was all but over. We were all but home. We proceeded sedately in tandem and we did not stop until we hit Cataby.

Tooling down through the Eneabba flats I thought about one last question for this trip. Is humankind a species that is worthwhile nurturing and protecting? I came to the conclusion that the dispassionate answer to this difficult question is "no". We behave fairly badly. Most animals of most types behave fairly badly of course. They fight and bully others to show their superiority and to show others of their type that they are of the best stock from which to breed. They kill for food to survive. They maraud against weaker animals or weaker groups of their own kind. They attach themselves to hosts and parasitically live off them. So they display many of the traits of humans but they do so without thought or malice.

Humankind does all these nasty things but there is a difference. Thinking and philosophical humans have worked out that these forms of behaviour are destructive and inimical to good relations between individuals and yet they are still common forms of behaviour. Humans do not need to fight for their existence as other forms of life do but this hangover from their past, apparently deeply embedded in their systems, causes them to still behave in a sad, dog eat dog way.

Bruce Chatwin has suggested that only nomadic peoples are truly happy and there could be some truth in that. But nomadic peoples still attacked each other and it is hard to believe that sedentary civilisation is the problem. So we come back to having to believe that the reasons humans behave badly is that it is an ineradicable part of their psyche. Is this good enough? Is the fact that Osama Bin Laden was an ascetic, desert Arab who devoutly believed in a monotheistic, militant God who will brook no other belief and insists that only He is followed, a good enough reason for the destruction of Yamasaki's World Trade Centre and the thousands in it who were wantonly killed? In my view it is not.

As I have already boasted I was twice fortunate enough to spend time with Minuro Yamasaki. I found him a quietly spoken, highly intelligent and humorous man and architect who was driven by an urge to excellence. He was not a man with the gigantic ego that so many great architects have possessed but behind the quiet demeanour was a steel core. I am grateful he did not live to see his great creations brought down by maniacal zealots in the name of their, all powerful God.

Humankind must now transcend these primal, destructive traits and some of its savage beliefs or it is doomed to a well earned extinction. I would like to believe that more thought and better education would lead us into paths of peace and prosperity but I was not optimistic as I rode along. I am still not as I laboriously type these words. Thoroughly gloomy with my thoughts and unhappy that the odyssey was nearly over I rode into Cataby and stopped for the last cup of coffee for the trip with my oldest and my youngest sons.

The break cheered me up. Nick and I reminisced about previous breaks at the road house on earlier trips north. I remembered stopping for a warming cup of coffee early one August morning when I rode the Turbo up to Port Denham. I was frozen. A few klicks up the track I was pinched for speeding. Later in the day I had to ride the 90km of loose sand up the Peron Peninsula on a bike not really made for that type of terrain. Much to my surprise I did not fall off.

Nick and I were reminded of the last leg of the journey around the north on the BMWs that we had made. I had a friend. Let's call him Newton to avoid any embarrassment and because that was his name. He wanted to meet us towards the end of our trip by riding his bike to a predetermined meeting place. We suggested Broome but he thought that was a bit far. Then we suggested Geraldton but that turned out to be a bit far also. Finally he settled on Cataby. We arrived there on time despite having come from Dongara. Newty was late. We waited and he finally turned up. After a coffee we hit the road. Newt' disappeared from our rear vision mirrors after a short while. Nick and I were not too worried. We were used to travelling at 140 per by that time and did not really expect him to keep up. However near Gin Gin we started to worry so we back tracked. Newt' had run out of petrol because he had failed to fill up at Cataby. He was a very clever bloke who ran a successful business, a nice bloke and a talented sailor but he did not have much of a future in long distance motor cycling on the form he showed on that ride.

We trundled down through the hills and across the flats through the vineyards and then we were home. We unpacked, unhitched the trailer and Hans drove Nick home. We all felt flat, even though it was good to be home.

Epilogue.

It was over but it will not be forgotten. I had had the company of my oldest and my youngest sons through a series of experiences, most of which were memorable and good. I had had the company of my dear wife in one of the most spectacular parts of the world. I had ridden 8000km to Kununurra and back but for a couple of short stints when Nick had the pleasure of the V4. I know that this was fairly self centred of me and a more generous soul would have shared the riding more with Nick but I contented myself with the thought that Nick will have many opportunities in the future whereas I am fast running out of time - or may be it is all over already.

What I can say without any equivocation is that the two sons who travelled with me are great travelling companions and I enjoyed their company a great deal. It is a pity that my other son, Ben, could not have joined us but he had other commitments and we could not have fitted our wives into the car for the Kununurra/El Questro/Argyle leg had he and his wife come. Will this really be my last long ride? Probably - but you never know. I might need another opportunity to clear my head and let my mind wander. I know I will want to see, once again, the clumps of Spinifex, the other poetic grasses of the Australian bush, Boab trees, termite mounds, and the wonders of Cape Keraudren, Purnululu Park, the Kimberley, the Hamersley Ranges and the wildflowers of the Gascoyne. We live in a magnificent country.

Whispering grasses.

Egotecture?
Art and function vs self-belief and salesmanship in architecture.
by
Peter Bruechle

Award winning buildings are now often extremely expensive and lack durability. They are unlikely to last long enough to enchant future generations, as the great buildings of the past enchant our generations.

Egotecture? presents a viewpoint suggesting that the icons of today's architecture are the result of critics who have not met their duties and, instead, have fallen for the self-belief of architects who possess incredible self-assurance and superb salesmanship. Their architecture is no longer a "practical art".

Read *Egotecture?* and see if you agree.

Issues and Challenges
Matters for consideration, discussion and consensus.
by
Peter Bruechle

"For peace and continuing development the world needs balanced and comprehensive education, not bigger and more destructive weapons of 'defence'."

Peter Bruechle's essays cover matters he considers need dispassionate discussion, not to assert the correctness of his opinions but to introduce them with the aim of provoking discussion that may lead to consensus.

Issues and Challenges is well-informed, thought-provoking, potentially controversial, and necessary in today's disturbed, volatile world.

www.ingramcontent.com/pod-product-compliance
Lightning Source LLC
Chambersburg PA
CBHW042053030526
44107CB00091B/1562